I bought this because it was such a good picture of you and Mavis on the cover!

sorry... it was a little sheepish!!!

Happy Birthday
Love
Jonathan Denise
Tess & crew
x x

PORTRAIT OF
THE NORTH YORK MOORS

By the same author

Constable across the Moors
Constable around the Village
Constable in the Dale
Constable on the Hill
Constable on the Prowl

Portrait of
THE NORTH YORK MOORS

by

Nicholas Rhea

ROBERT HALE · LONDON

First published in Great Britain 1985

ISBN 0 7090 2276 X

Robert Hale Limited
Clerkenwell House
Clerkenwell Green
London EC1R 0HT

British Library Cataloguing in Publication Data

Rhea, Nicholas
Portrait of the North York Moors.
1. North York Moors (England)—Description and travel
I. Title
914.28′4604858 DA670.Y6

ISBN 0-7090-2276-X

Photoset in North Wales by
Derek Doyle & Associates, Mold, Clwyd.
Printed in Great Britain by
St Edmundsbury Press, Bury St Edmunds, Suffolk.
Bound by Woolnough Bookbinding Limited.

Contents

For my family

List of Illustrations

PICTURE CREDITS

The North Yorkshire County Librarian (The Bertram Unné Collection): 1,5,7-11,20,23-4,26,42,45; John Fawcett: 2-3,6,12,16,21,41,43-4; John Tindale: 4,15,17,22,25,27,30-7,39,40,46; The North York Moors National Park: 13-14,18,28,38; Youth Hostels Association/P. Westwood: 19; The Editor, *Darlington and Stockton Times*: 29

Acknowledgements

I wish to record my thanks and gratitude to the following, who helped in various ways with the preparation of this book:

The County Librarian and staff of the North Yorkshire County Library at Northallerton for allowing me access to the valuable Bertram Unné Collection of Photographs, and for granting me permission to reproduce the following prints from that collection: the Cleveland Hills from Swainby Bank; Mount Grace Priory; Roseberry Topping; one of the Bridestones from Allerston High Moor; Farndale from Blakey Ridge in the background; the Hole of Horcum; Banniscue and Easterside, near Hawnby; St Gregory's Minster, Kirkdale; Rosedale; Lilla Cross; Guisborough Priory; Sutton Bank and Lake Gormire; Rievaulx Abbey.

The North York Moors National Park Officer and staff at Helmsley for permission to reproduce the following prints: a grouse butt; Staindale Lake in Dalby Forest; a woodland footpath near Grosmont; Newton Dale showing the track of the North York Moors Railway; the Moors Centre, formerly, the North York Moors National Park Information Centre, Danby Lodge.

The Youth Hostels Association for the photograph of Wheeldale Youth Hostel.

The Editor of the *Darlington and Stockton Times* for allowing me to reproduce without charge the photograph of Little Fryup Dale.

John Tindale of Whitby for searching his files and allowing me to reproduce the following prints: aerial view of the Ballistic Missile Early Warning Station at Fylingdales; Danby-in-Cleveland; Beggar's Bridge, Glaisdale; the scene following the floods of 1930 between Glaisdale and Egton Bridge; Whitby at night; Sandsend showing the railway viaduct; planting of the Penny Hedge; aerial view of Whitby; Eskdaleside; HM The Queen's Ascot landau drawn by Cleveland Bays; Ravenscar;

girls wearing Staithes bonnets; Staithes at low tide; Mallyan Spout waterfall; a moorland farm; World Champion gooseberry; Caedmon's Cross, Whitby.

John Fawcett of Harrogate for his photographs of the Star Inn, Harome; Shandy Hall, Coxwold; Sun Inn, Bilsdale; Ampleforth Abbey; the Austin Wright sculpture; Mauley Cross; the Roman road on Wheeldale Moor; Hutton-le-Hole; the view across Cropton Forest.

John Fawcett also took the cover photograph of Glaisdale Dale.

In addition, I wish to thank everyone who responded to my letters, telephone calls and conversations about aspects of the North York Moors. They are too numerous to thank individually but their contribution was invaluable.

And deep gratitude goes to Mrs Pat Leigh, who sorted out my jumble of notes and typed this manuscript so well.

* * *

'The countie of Yorke was in the Saxon tongue called Evona-Yeyne and now commonly Yorkshire, farr greater and more numerous in the circuit of her miles than any shire in England.

'Shee is much bound to the singular love and motherly care of nature, in placing her under so temperate a clime, that in every measure she be indifferently fruitfull.

'If one part of her be stony, and a sandy, barren ground; another is fertile and richly adorned with cornefields.

'If you here finde it naked and destitute of woods, you shall see it there shadowed with forrests full of trees, that have very thicke bodies, sending forth many fruitfull and profitable branches.

'If one place of it be moorish, mirie and unpleasant, another makes a free tender of delight and presents it selfe to the eye, full of beautie and contentive variety.'

John Speed, 1627

1

Introduction

God made the country and man made the town.
William Cowper (1731–1800)

Ten minutes pleasurable walk from my home is a hilltop which in times past bore an ancient beacon. It is on a route used by long-extinct tribes, then by the Romans and drovers who trekked from Scotland with foot-weary cattle. Now it carries modern travellers about their business and pleasure. It affords glorious and expansive views across North Yorkshire to the distant Dales and Pennines, to the gentle Wolds of East Yorkshire and to the romantic and spectacular North York Moors.

The huge block of land which in its entirety is called the North York Moors really comprises a collection of smaller moors, all bearing names. There are almost 150 of them, and in addition the Moors include a stretch of coastline and over one hundred deep valleys called dales as well as many villages and hamlets. About forty per cent of the North York Moors is open moorland.

Within the parent Moors, each minor moor is an individual patch of land with its own identity.

One difficulty in presenting all these smaller moors is that few of them have clearly defined boundaries. They fuse with their neighbours through invisible lines, and indeed some tiny moors

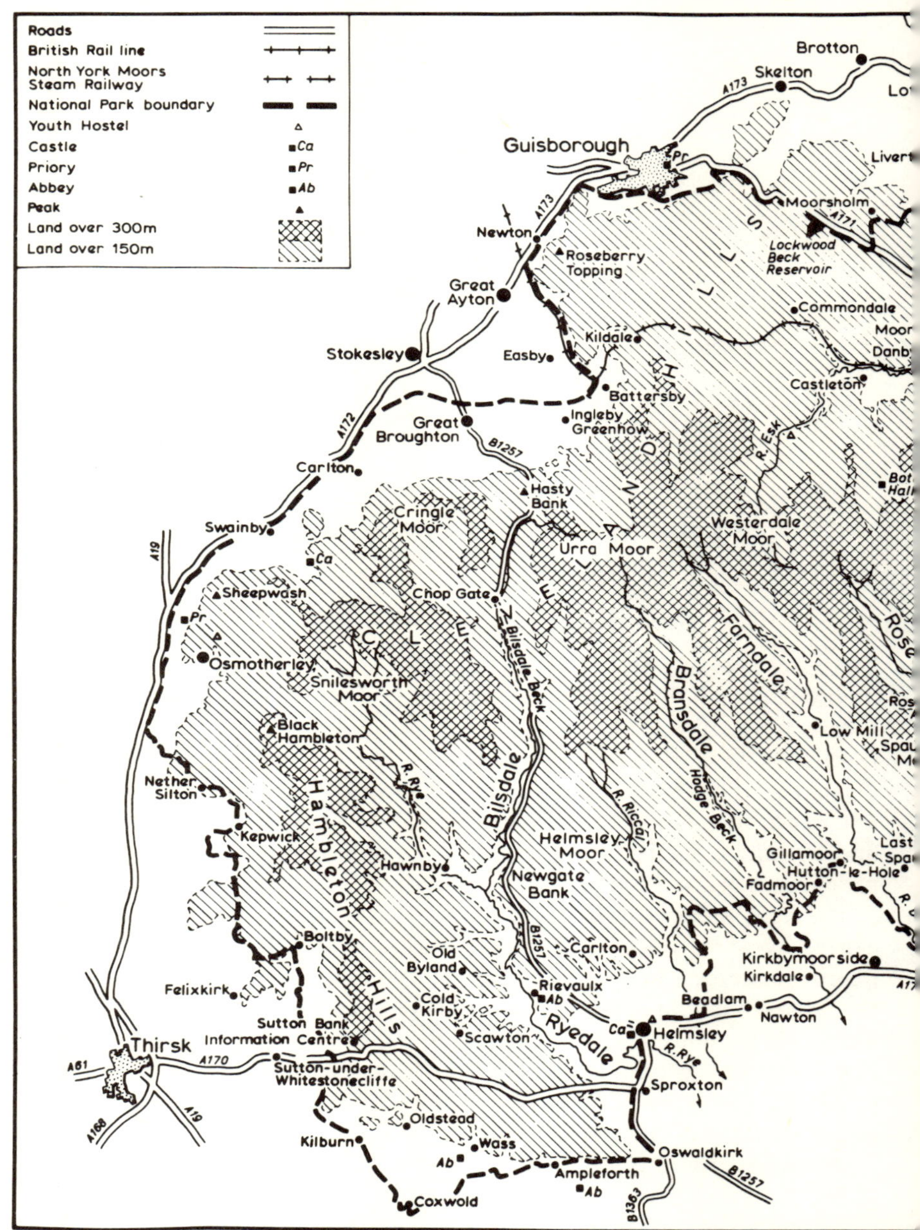

Roads
British Rail line
North York Moors Steam Railway
National Park boundary
Youth Hostel
Castle
Priory
Abbey
Peak
Land over 300m
Land over 150m
Brotton
Skelton
A173
Guisborough
Pr
Moorsholm
A171
Lockwood Beck Reservoir
Newton
A173
Roseberry Topping
Great Ayton
Commondale
Stokesley
Easby
Kildale
Castleton
Battersby
Ingleby Greenhow
Great Broughton
A172
B1257
R. Esk
Carlton
Hasty Bank
Cringle Moor
Westerdale Moor
Swainby
Urra Moor
A19
Ca
Sheepwash
Chop Gate
Pr
Osmotherley
Snilesworth Moor
Farndale
Bilsdale Beck
Bransdale
Black Hambleton
Low Mill
R. Rye
Nether Silton
Bilsdale
R. Riccal
Hodge Beck
Hambleton
Kepwick
Helmsley Moor
Gillamoor
Hutton-le-Hole
Hawnby
Newgate Bank
Fadmoor
B1257
Carlton
Boltby
Kirkbymoorside
Old Byland
Kirkdale
Felixkirk
Hills
Rievaulx
Ab
Beadlam
Cold Kirby
Nawton
Sutton Bank Information Centre
Ryedale
Ca
Helmsley
Thirsk
Scawton
R. Rye
A61
A170
Sutton-under-Whitestonecliffe
Sproxton
A168
A19
Oldstead
Kilburn
Wass
Oswaldkirk
Ab
Ampleforth
B1257
Ab
Coxwold
B1363

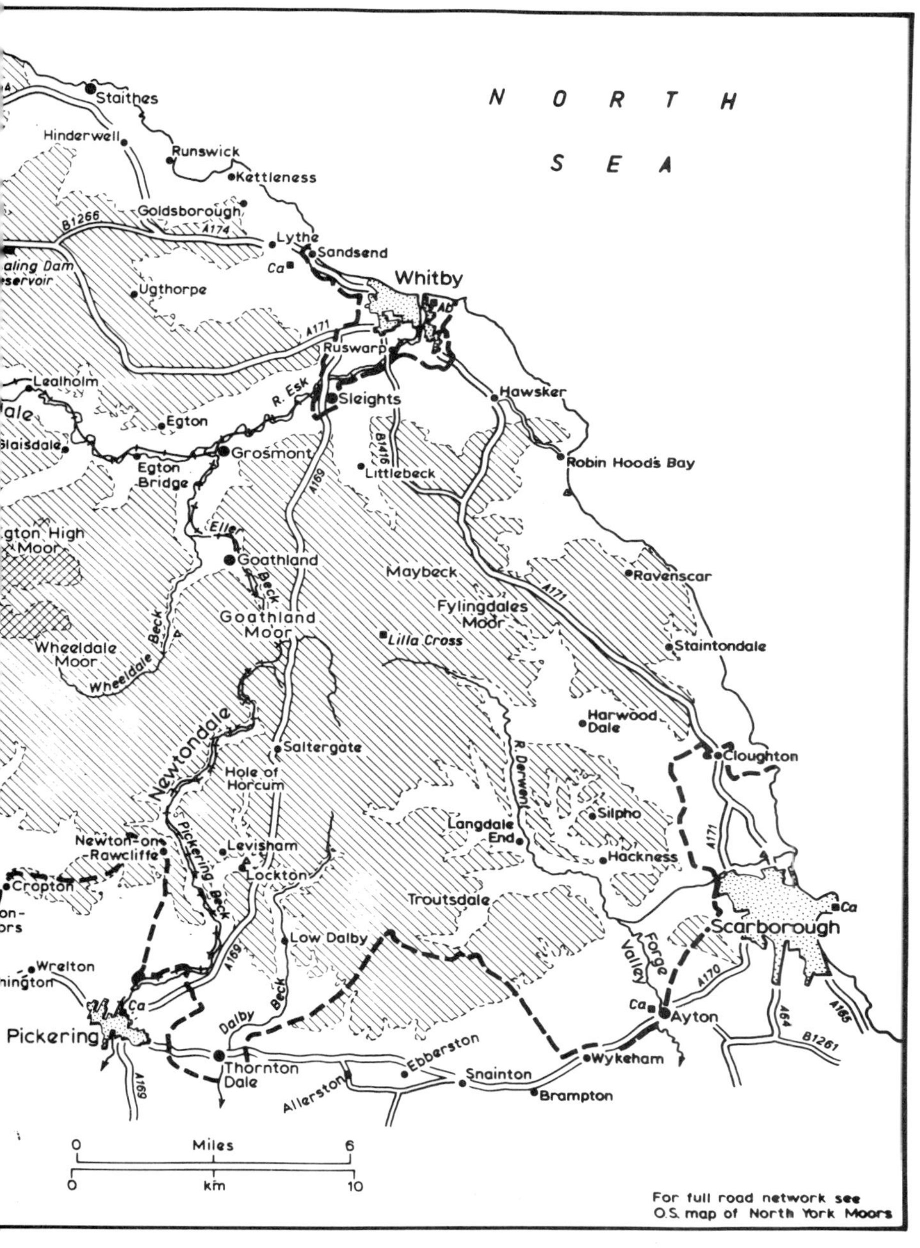
N O R T H
S E A
Staithes
Hinderwell
Runswick
Kettleness
Goldsborough
B1266
A174
Lythe
Sandsend
Ca
Whitby
Ab
Ugthorpe
A171
Ruswarp
Lealholm
R. Esk
Sleights
Hawsker
Egton
Grosmont
B1416
Littlebeck
Robin Hood's Bay
Egton
Bridge
A169
Eller
Goathland
Beck
Maybeck
Ravenscar
A171
Fylingdales
Moor
Goathland
Moor
Lilla Cross
Staintondale
Wheeldale
Moor
Wheeldale
Beck
Newtondale
Harwood
Dale
Saltergate
R. Derwent
Cloughton
Hole of
Horcum
Silpho
Langdale
End
A171
Newton-on-
Rawcliffe
Levisham
Pickering Beck
Hackness
Lockton
Cropton
Troutsdale
Ca
Scarborough
Low Dalby
A169
Forge
Valley
Wrelton
A170
Ca
Ayton
Ca
Dalby
Beck
A64
A165
Pickering
B1261
Ebberston
Wykeham
Thornton
Dale
Snainton
A169
Allerston
Brampton
0
Miles
6
0
km
10
For full road network see
O.S. map of North York Moors

lie snug within the bosoms of larger ones. Tucked between Rosedale Moor and Wheeldale Moor, for example, is Hamer Moor, with the baby White Moor fighting for space alongside. It gets more confusing when we learn that the small Ingleby Moor is part of the larger Baysdale Moor, itself an expanse within the Cleveland Hills which in turn are a section of the North York Moors.

Try to think of the whole area as a rosebed. An exquisite rosebed can contain hundreds of blooms; together they create one unit but individually they are gorgeous flowers in their own right, all with their own identity and character. At a distance, those characteristics can disappear, because the rosebed is viewed as a whole. As one approaches, though, individual variations can be seen and understood without any detraction from the overall beauty. At very close quarters, however, some of those lovely roses will be imperfect and their thorns will present hazards.

The Moors are like that. At a distance, they are beautiful and fascinating, with an overriding sense of space and freedom, but at close quarters the characteristics of each minor moor become evident and respected; and, as with the roses, there will be imperfections and even danger.

In recognition of the fact that the North York Moors are an area of outstanding natural beauty, they were declared a National Park in 1952, one of two National Parks based in North Yorkshire. The other is the Yorkshire Dales National Park in the Pennine region.

The area of the Moors National Park is 553 square miles (1,432 square kilometres), and a map of this portion of Yorkshire looks surprisingly like an outline of Australia.

The term 'National Park' still confuses some, who believe it is owned by the nation. Indeed, most of the land within the Moors is privately owned, albeit with some fifteen hundred miles of public footpaths. The purpose of the National Park is to enhance our appreciation of the countryside, to preserve natural beauty and to respect those who live and work in the area.

This book therefore seeks to portray the beauties that lie within the North York Moors National Park, as well as those which lie around but adjacent to the Park's boundaries. It will be like looking at a map of the National Park with a halo about it!

With these fluid horizons in mind, it is possible to divide the Moors into smaller areas, such as (1) the coast; (2) the Cleveland Hills which lie to the north and north-west and which have variously been called Blackamor, Blakemoor or Blackamoor; (3) the Hambleton Hills which are on the western edge and (4) the Tabular Hills which form the south and south-east of the Moors, some of which are afforested. The Howardian Hills, nominated in the autumn of 1984 as an area of outstanding natural beauty, lie beyond the southern boundary of the National Park. Within those divisions are the 150 smaller moors, and in very general terms the Cleveland Hills, named after the Norsemen's Klifland, lie to the north and north-west of Eskdale. Its river flows from west to east, the only one in the Moors to do so. The Hambleton Hills occupy the high ground on the west of Bilsdale. Its rivers Seph and Rye run to the south, while the central portion, whose several rivers drop from the moors into Ryedale, can be regarded as the Tabular Hills, so called because of their remarkably flat appearance.

The main routes across the Moors are contiguous to these natural divisions. For example, as it crosses the Moors north of Eskdale, the A171 from Guisborough to Whitby follows the hilltop line of that valley and then follows the coast to Scarborough; the B1257 from Stokesley to Helmsley makes use of Bilsdale, while the A169 from Whitby to Pickering runs from the north to the south like the rivers in the Tabular Hills. A point of interest along this road is Saltersgate Inn, a remote moorland hotel whose peat fire has burned for 170 years, once used for making hot buttered turf cakes. The inn was once the haunt of smugglers, and one is said to be buried under the hearth which contains the famous peat fire.

There are two railways on the Moors: the scenic Whitby to Middlesbrough British Rail line follows Eskdale's tortuous valley route, while the Grosmont to Pickering line, a picturesque privately run steam railway called the North York Moors Railway, makes use of Newton Dale and the Valley of the Murk Esk as it follows the general route of the A169. This line crosses a bog in Newton Dale, and to create a base for his track in the 1830s, George Stephenson laid a platform of brushwood, timber and sheeps' fleeces filled with heather.

With so few railways and main highways, communication

within the main bulk of the Moors is achieved through many minor and unclassified roads, some with extraordinarily steep and narrow inclines.

The gradient of one in three (thirty-three per cent) is not uncommon and until recently was seldom announced by a road sign because it is not out of the ordinary. Examples can be experienced by driving through Littlebeck or down Chimney Bank at Rosedale or up White Horse Bank at Kilburn. Some of these roads stretch high into the Moors to end their lives in farmyards, while others trek across the heights to link one dale with the next, and to provide tourists with staggering views. Several are forbidden to coaches. In the summer, the views are truly breathtaking; in the depths of winter, those roads can be treacherous when they are not blocked by deep drifts.

This dearth of main roads arises because there are no towns within the Moors. Whitby and Scarborough sit beyond the heather and outside the National Park, as do the others which ring the Moors. These are typical North Yorkshire market towns with thriving open-air markets, and all stand back from the boundaries of the Park; they are Loftus and Guisborough, both now in County Cleveland, and the North Yorkshire towns of Stokesley, Thirsk, Kirkbymoorside and Pickering, with Malton a short distance away. Helmsley has the National Park's boundary running through its centre.

My vantage point on that beacon overlooks much of this, but it is not the highest point of the Moors, nor even the best vantage point or their most beautiful or historic site, though it does provide a dramatic vista and more than a hint of concealed pleasures.

Every morning, I journey on foot to that beacon. It provides the very best of nature, an oft-changing scene as I exercise my heart, lungs, legs and mind. My eyes and ears feast upon the sights and sounds of the breathtaking countryside, and I thank God for the wonders He has made so freely available to mankind.

I am proud that this inspirational walk begins my working day. To start one's daily toil fortified by the touch of nature and such unfettered views is indeed a privilege.

There are times when the bleating of new-born lambs accompanies me, when the harsh call of the magpie sounds nearby, when long-tailed tits eye me from the security of a hawthorn hedge, when a grey squirrel runs beside me or a hare sprints for cover. On that short walk, I have seen badgers lumber across the lane; there have been nervous deer and sly foxes, flocks of cheeky starlings and charms of handsome goldfinches, brave or silly pheasants and bewildered moles, the song of the blackbird and the constant rustle of moorland breezes. I have seen rabbits and rooks, voles and weasels, harvest mice, skylarks and partridge, cuckoos and kestrels and more besides.

This short climb supports hedgerows which include a tumble of white and pink roses, wild gooseberries, plums and apples; there is honeysuckle, valerian and sloes, briars, hawthorn and elderberries, wild lilac and wild mint, vetches and cow parsley, celandines and primroses, with maple and massive oaks, all surrounded by open fields with the purple moors reclining at a discreet distance.

There are oddities too, like black rabbits and contrasting white pheasants, both naturally wild in this countryside.

These and the views are all part of that short walk.

And, as if to remind me of one aspect of the history of the Moors, I am frequently accompanied by the deep, booming notes of Gregory John, the huge bell of the Abbey of St Lawrence, out of sight in the valley. It calls the monks to a daily Mass in the manner of distant times, and when the valley is shrouded in mist or coated with newly fallen snow, that sonorous bell provides a curious and even mystical sense of companionship. It is not difficult to appreciate the value of medieval bells which guided weary travellers to shelter. It is a comforting sound.

But it is the Moors which command my attention. They glow rich and purple in the autumn as the glorious heather smothers the heights with a mass of flowers, while in winter they look superlative in their covering of pure white snow. They resemble all that is fresh and clean, a vast expanse of virgin territory, but they are lethal to those unfamiliar with their black moods and wintering terrain.

Having been born deep in their midst and having then worked in them and around them all my life, I know there is treachery among that beauty. Each new season brings its own risks – there are the snows of winter, the mists of autumn, the fires of summer and the uncertainty of spring.

These are a feature of life which the moorland folk endure and respect. Each new winter presents a test of survival, not only for the farmer in his isolated farmstead but for the creatures which occupy those heights. Some are domesticated like the free-roaming black-faced sheep, some are pursued for the food of man, like the grouse, and yet more live in the wild freedom that nature provides. There is the curlew and the hare, the fox and the stoat. The stoat adapts to the winter by donning a coat of white to disguise his brown presence, while birds like the wheatear or swallow solve their problems by flying off to warmer places.

The heather and also the sphagnum moss which softens the toughness of the landscape both survive beneath the snow, but the exposed, windswept heights discourage the growth of trees and in places recline beneath a blanket of thick, troublesome bracken.

But it is not all sombre and forbidding. Each new spring clothes the dales with green and paints them with an array of brilliant wild flowers and blossom, some common and some rare. Rushing moorland streams cascade over jagged rocks to bring a welcome freshness to the countryside, and to complement the pretty stone villages, ancient churches, abbeys, ruined castles and well-kept greens.

Then summer draws human visitors to witness another seasonal transformation. There are times when the treeless heights shimmer in the heat of midday, when lizards and adders bask on the rocks, when the becks which flow from the peat fade into mere trickles of brown water. It is then that the Moors are so vulnerable to fire. Many fires begin by carelessness; they kill the birds, animals and plants, they ruin the heather and the peat upon which depend so many lives, animal and human.

There are times when the valley floors are rich with man-made crops or dancing with the trumpets of the wild daffodils or the pretty yellow of cowslips and primroses; when dense green woodlands shimmer with the deep azure haze of the bluebell, and the hedgerows are thick with wild roses.

Amid this timeless beauty, I am reminded of the twentieth century by the distant sight of the three white radomes of Fylingdales Ballistic Missile Early Warning Station, a futuristic peace-keeping edifice whose mysteries are enclosed in that clutch of three giant white eggs. From my vantage point, more than twenty miles away, they look like huge, smooth duck eggs in a moorland nest of purple heather. The flat-topped heights which accommodate those eggs also appear smooth and unadventurous.

But I know this is not so. Those Moors and their deep valleys are one of the last unexplored and unexploited regions of England. There is no industry and no urbanization; there is just human bliss among the contentment of nature.

Growing to maturity in the Moors, I learned of the stirring countryside and landscape around me; I learned of the people, the history, the legends and superstitions, the dialect, folklore and character, the wildlife and vegetation, the beauty and the constant appeal of the Moors. As a child, I thought everyone had access to such delights; it was a long time before I realized I was privileged both to live in such surroundings and to benefit from the experience and inherent commonsense and wisdom of the moorland folk, coupled with their capacity for sustained hard work.

My childhood home was Glaisdale, a village which sprawls across the end of a deep, broad valley cultivated along its floor but surrounded on high by the bleak, open Moors.

I was brought up with tales of the Hart Hall Hob and of witches who were deterred by witch posts. I loved the romantic tale of Tom Ferris who fought with Drake against the Spanish Armada and who returned in 1619 to build Beggar's Bridge, over which I walked to school.

I became fascinated by the rapid-flowing waters of the River Esk and learned they were born at the attractively named Esklets high on the moors. They flow past Danby Castle, home of one of the wives of Henry VIII, and that river, which remains free from pollution, harbours succulent salmon and trout as it rushes through dramatic gorges to Egton Bridge. This tiny village is renowned for its staunch adherence to the Roman Catholic faith, an ancient faith which survived the Reformation and produced the saintly martyr Father Nicholas Postgate. Egton Bridge also produced the world's largest gooseberry and still features its annual Gooseberry Show.

Those same clear waters of the Esk flow into the North Sea at Whitby; they carried Captain James Cook to discover Australia.

And they flowed below the flourishing abbey of Streonshalh, now called Whitby, the home of Caedmon, England's first poet, the pride of St Hilda and scene of a synod in AD 664 which determined the method for calculating the date of Easter. That system still applies.

Close to my village is Arncliffe Wood, a place of enchantment for a growing boy. There I spent hours watching green woodpeckers and nuthatches or searching for the cave of Robin Hood. According to local legend, the wood contains a secret underground passage which connects with distant Robin Hood's Bay. I never did find that cave.

I walked in circles upon the Wishing Stone, a large, square rock with a tree growing from its centre as I made childhood wishes. We believed it was lucky to walk three times around the tree, dreaming unspoken dreams.

The wood contained splendid grey beech and sweet chestnut trees and was often carpeted with bluebells, primroses and cowslips, but there was also the awesome Lovers' Leap. Local talk said lovers long ago had ended their short, unhappy lives by leaping down the cliff into the turbulent Esk and that a man had drowned in the nearby Dead Man's Pool.

A sense of reality is maintained by the single-line railway which still weaves between the trees and follows the twisting route of the river. As it wends its way down this narrow dale, it crosses and re-crosses the river on a series of sturdy bridges. British Rail diesels now pass that way, but from that clifftop vantage point I would watch the smart green steam-engines of the LNER (London and North Eastern Railway) as they tugged their trains along this most picturesque of routes, rattling across the metal bridge which spans the deep gorge below Lovers' Leap. Sometimes an LMS (London, Midland and Scottish) engine in its maroon livery would call this way. Occasionally I would walk along the line, over that bridge, terrified that I would slip between the gaping timbers to crash into the turbulent river below. Downstream today, steam trains hiss along the North York Moors Railway, so popular that there is talk of its being extended into Whitby.

Beside the Esk as it flowed through the wood, it was possible to hide among the dense greenery to watch herons or otters at play, to see otter cubs sliding down their mud-paths into the river, and their parents feeding on salmon by taking a single, sharp bite from the back of the neck. Kingfishers skimmed the surface in a flash of brilliant blue, sandpipers hunted along the banks, and sand martins built their nests in the higher places. Wild bees worked upon the floral decorations of the wood as glowworms and wild strawberries graced the side of that railway track, with rhododendrons adorning the woodland floor.

As I matured, some of that magic evaporated, but not all. I learned of the vanished ironstone industry of my own village, of bygone bursts of jet mining, of attempts to build railways through impossible places and of the roads that came late to these lonely hills. These enterprises demanded hard work, but they provided employment for the people of the dales, for men and women already accustomed to working hard for their daily living. The local hill farmers continue to eke a tough, hardy living from the moors, some with never a day off and never a holiday away from the district.

Two World Wars passed over the Moors, and one lasting memory is of the first German plane of World War II to be shot down over England. The successful pilot was Group Captain Peter Townsend, a friend of HRH Princess Margaret in later life, and the plane was brought down near Sleights.

If this was a 'first' in aerial battle, another first was scored long ago, when the Moors witnessed the first-ever flight by a man, an occasion constantly and perhaps unfairly overshadowed by more publicized aviators.

There are treasures ancient and modern within these Moors, and I hope the following notes will enable them to be shared by others. It is to be hoped that neither progress nor the visitor will ever destroy this charming corner of the British Isles, for it is the home and workplace of many, including myself.

This, then, is my Portrait of a very special part of Yorkshire.

2

The people discover the Moors

Man hath all that nature hath – but more.
Matthew Arnold (1822–88)

Some 250 million years ago, the landscape we now know as the North York Moors began to take shape. It is possible that the low-lying areas were under warm water which would be shallow in some places and very deep in others. There is even a possibility that at one stage the entire district was submerged and that the higher ranges of land could have produced an archipelago, a scene readily visualized when roaming the Moors; and about 80 million years ago dinosaurs roamed the land, and winged reptiles flew across the heights where the grouse now clatters from the heather. In time, the mass of vegetation generated by that mild climate began to rot, and this formed the basis of coal, peat and oil which have subsequently been found and extracted.

The Moors were then a network of lakes, the largest of which (if it still existed) might be called Lake Pickering. Had it survived, it could have been England's largest lake, some thirty-two miles long by eight miles wide at its broadest point. In addition, the many dales which push into the Moors would have each contained a smaller lake to provide the ingredients by which life could be supported and sustained. The following lakes, named after present-day dales, are known to have existed – Lake Eskdale, Lake Glaisdale, Lake Wheeldale, Lake Scugdale, Lake Kildale and Lake Rosedale. In addition, there was Lake Gormire, which remains as the region's largest natural lake, but as the others receded, they left behind rich deposits of fertile earth.

Even today, those dales benefit from that rich beginning, for they are fertile, green and lush, and at times their formative years can be recalled when the saturated earth glistens with the retained waters of winter. It is not difficult to imagine those valleys full of shimmering, clear water.

The present landscape probably took shape within the last two million years or so, for it is since that time that the earth has suffered a series of Ice Ages. These were viciously cold periods interspaced with spells of surprising warmth, but each of them carpeted the landscape with a thick layer of ice. This resulted in shifting glaciers sculpting the distinctive dales and hills from areas which had once been lakes.

The most recent Ice Age began some seventy thousand years ago and lasted for about sixty thousand years. It is now known that around the beginning of that final Ice Age the Moors were the home of some surprising animals. Their remains indicate that between the Ice Ages the temperature was sub-tropical and that vegetation more in keeping with the jungle existed within the Moors.

Evidence of these beasts was unexpectedly discovered in March 1821. While quarrying at Kirkdale, near Kirkbymoorside, within sight of the ancient Minster of St Gregory, a workman found the mouth of a cave. It was in a cliff-face several feet above ground-level, and it remains visible from the road which crosses the ford near St Gregory's Minster, Kirkdale. When he peered inside, the workman found the bones of many animals, which he threw away – some went into the river below. They were not important to him – they were simply old bones.

Fortunately, they were noticed by a Mr John Gibson, on holiday in Helmsley. He appreciated their tremendous importance, and through the efforts of Doctor John Harrison and some local antiquaries, the leading palaeontologist of the last century, the Reverend Dr W. Buckland, was persuaded to examine them. He quickly realized this was a unique find, and his examination showed that the heavily gnawed bones were the remains of animals which had lived some seventy thousand years before Christ. Furthermore, they came from species which no longer lived wild in the British Isles and showed that England, or at least this corner of it, had once enjoyed a warm and probably sub-tropical climate.

The bones included those of the lion, tiger, hippopotamus, bison, giant deer, straight-tusked elephant and slender-nosed rhinoceros. In addition, the discovery of some three hundred hyena bones led Dr Buckland to believe the cave had once been a hyenas' den. Lack of any complete skeleton supported this theory, because the hyena gnaws the bones of its prey and eats its own dead.

A thick layer of internal sediment suggested the area around Pickering had once been a massive lake, with this ancient lair on its shores. The cave mouth is now some 175 feet above sea-level (but only a few feet above ground-level), and it is known that, at times, the lake surface reached 250 feet above sea-level. Thus the cave would occasionally be flooded, but when the waters finally receded, they left the cave high above the floor of the vanished lake with its entrance sealed.

The species known to have been in the Kirkdale Cave, both when the district was warm and when it was cold, include the wolf, fox, brown bear, cave bear, stoat, lion, spotted hyena, mouse, water vole, Abbot's vole, short-tailed field vole, brown hare, rabbit, slender-nosed rhinoceros, woolly rhinoceros, horse, pig, hippopotamus, reindeer, red deer, giant deer, European bison, wild ox, straight-tusked elephant and mammoth. The animals from the 'warm' period include the hippopotamus, bison and giant deer, while those from the 'cold' period include the mammoth, woolly rhinoceros, reindeer and horse.

This remarkable collection of relics has been distributed among several museums, but many have been lost for ever. Some were mixed with local road-making materials!

There is a local theory and some evidence that a large and complicated system of caves exists below this limestone region. Wheels of farm vehicles have sunk into underground passages, while land movement and subsidence continue to suggest that more caves await discovery. One story says a goose made its way from the Kirkdale Cave into Kirkbymoorside by travelling two miles underground, losing all its feathers in the process!

If more caves are found, perhaps more bones, or artefacts, will be revealed and we might learn more about our very early history.

But one puzzle remains. Did man ever see this cave or enter it? Did he set eyes on any of those strange beasts? We may never know, for there is no evidence that man set foot inside the Kirkdale Cave until that workman found it in 1821.

It is known that humans of the New Stone Age came to the Moors within the last ten thousand years. They lived on the Cleveland Hills during the Mesolithic Age, long before the Neolithic Age, the Bronze Age and the Iron Age. Short in stature, with dark complexions and hair, they had ancestors in the Mediterranean regions and were European in appearance. Some remnants of these features remain in the moorland folk and fisher people of the Moors and coast. By the arrival of the Neolithic period, they had learned to make tools and cultivate the earth. They could produce pottery and were able to spin wool and weave cloth. Furthermore, they bred cattle and grew cereals, though in their time the moors were coated with trees.

It is known that around 8000 BC the Moors enjoyed a liberal covering of deciduous forest, a picture not easily visualized when looking across today's bleak heights. There was oak, birch, beech, hazel, elm, willow and lime. These were used for fuel and for a variety of other domestic purposes, including shelter for people and animals. But as man cultivated the Moors for his crops, the woodland vanished, and a lack of knowledgeable husbandry led to heather and moss taking over. In time, the Moors became a vast, empty area of bleak, treeless heights smothered in heather and bracken, a situation that endured for centuries. Oddly enough, that situation is now being reversed in some places as heather is being removed and the land re-cultivated or afforested. In some places, bracken is usurping the heather.

Many relics of early man's presence on the Moors have been found and can still be seen. The earliest are probably those discovered in 1949 at Star Carr, near Seamer, Scarborough, close to the edge of what might have been a small lake or even a bay of Lake Pickering. The discovery suggests these people had been lakeside dwellers with shelters built on platforms of birch, and the find revealed domestic waste, some animal remains and a number of flints. These people had burned the forest to clear the land for cultivation and were probably of the Mesolithic or Middle Stone Age.

Most of the ancient inhabited sites are above the thousand-foot mark, and some date to 5000 BC. Evidence of these moorland dwellers is shown by as many as three thousand barrows, large burial chambers which are among the oldest type of funeral mound in England. The Moors' horizons are repeatedly broken by these long, low mounds, many of which would have contained up to a dozen bodies. The larger of these are known locally as howes, some dating to the New Stone Age (3000–1800 BC) and others to the Bronze Age (1800–500 BC). Excavations have shown that some bore signs of burning, suggesting cremation, and one account suggests that more than ten thousand barrows once existed on the Moors.

The full extent of the Neolithic occupancy of the Moors is uncertain, for there is no clear distinction between the disappearance of one culture and the arrival of another.

New Stone Age Man arrived around 3000 BC. His attempts at settlement cleared more areas of existing forest, and very gradually the whole of the high moorland was colonized. Considerable numbers lived there and grazed their cattle, goats and sheep. (The tradition of grazing sheep on the Moors has continued and remains a vital part of the local economy.) As in earlier cultures, their presence prevented the forest re-establishing itself, and any surviving trees were felled for fuel, although the valleys remained heavily, or even densely, afforested. In all, the Moors endured about a thousand years of heavy grazing, and as the people gradually cleared and cultivated the valleys and then moved into them, the encroaching heather was free to establish itself.

When man began to fashion his implements from metal instead of stone, a new era began: this was the Bronze Age. But within the Moors flint continued to be used for tools and weapons long after the Bronze Age had established itself. The Bronze Age culture survived for about seventeen hundred years, albeit with differing cultures functioning alongside. It was perhaps the isolated nature of the Moors and the barren hills, with their deep pockets of productive landscape, that separated one group from another and allowed them all to survive unmolested. No doubt the nomadic lifestyle of some tribes contributed to this.

Because much of the low land was marshy and thickly overgrown with trees and vegetation, it deterred all but the most adventurous. It was the heights that remained open and provided the means of communication, because many tracks crossed and re-crossed the Moors, some fortified with trenches or mounds to protect the travellers. Evidence of these trenches has been found on Egton High Moor and Westerdale Moor, and in Fryup Dale and Danby Dale. Some of them extended miles to the south, well into the Howardian Hills near the present site of Castle Howard, since made famous as 'Brideshead', in the TV adaptation of *Brideshead Revisited.*

Next to settle on and around the Moors were the Celts, a tall, powerful and brave race who conquered much of northern Europe – among their conquests was England. They could fashion iron and cast it into tools and weapons such as swords and knives, and their heavy ploughs with iron blades could turn the tough earth of the Moors. Their religion caused them to worship natural objects like springs, wells and streams.

Those who lived north of Pickering, however, did not bury their dead, and a Greek traveller, Pythias, who came this way in 325 BC, noticed severed heads around the Celtic villages. It seems they regarded the human head as a symbol of their faith, and some were thrown into wells as a protection against evil.

During the early years of the first century, the Moors and other parts of the north of England were inhabited by a powerful, wandering but civilized Celtic tribe known as the Brigantes. They had a king and queen, and their own gold coinage. They fell into two clear classes. One group was wealthy and warlike; the men wore armour fashioned from leather and chain with bronze breastplates and magnificent plumed helmets. They carried blue shields to distinguish them from the other tribes and in times of peace wore tartans and trousers fastened tightly around the ankles. They were warriors who successfully used swords, knives, spears and even darts in battle. The famous trident depicted in popular portrayals of Britannia is said to have been copied from their pikes. The other branch was less well-to-do. They lived primitively on the Moors, scratching a tough living by rearing sheep and cattle. They wore animal skins and lived in small huts, sometimes isolated and sometimes in a village community with small fields around them. Those who worked as shepherds lived on the Moors, and it seems they never learned to grow crops or make cheese. Meat appears to have been their main diet.

The Brigantes were occupying the Moors when the Romans invaded England in 55 BC. The first wave of Romans did not reach the Moors; the second, which arrived in AD 43, concerned itself with the south and south-east of England, and then in AD 47–8 the Roman Governor of Britain, Ostorius Scapula, headed north towards Chester. He tried to reach an agreement with the Brigantes of that region, but this divided them into those who supported the Romans and those who resisted them.

The anti-Roman Brigantes, led by King Venutius, settled on the slopes of Ingleborough in the Yorkshire Pennines, where he moulded his men into an efficient fighting force. He knew that sooner or later the Romans would attack, so he built a fort at Stanwick, near Richmond. In AD 74, even before his fort was complete, the Roman legions attacked and killed Venutius. His people scattered, leaving the Romans dominant on the Moors.

Nearby York became their most important city in England, from both a military and a commercial point of view. They erected splendid buildings, and York became known as Altera Roma, the Alternative or Second Rome. It was capital of the northern province known as Maxima Caesariensis, a seat of government, a centre of communications and a military headquarters. Its territory stretched from Hadrian's Wall in the north to the River Humber in the south, and therefore included the North York Moors.

Even with their splendid capital so close at hand, it is feasible that small pockets of the Moors were never completely dominated by the Romans, though they did live and work on the moorland heights. They came from Lincolnshire, probably crossing the huge Humber estuary by ferry and following a route across the Wolds. This would bring them to the area now known as Malton and Norton, twin towns which straddle the River Derwent below the southern edge of the Moors. Here was the location of an important Roman settlement called Derventio where the Emperor Trajan (AD 90–117) established his fort. It had stone walls ten feet thick which were defended by two outer ditches.

Although Malton was important, the Romans also settled at Whorlton, Guisborough and Whitby, with a presence in the Cleveland Hills and parts of Ryedale. A Roman site is currently under examination near Helmsley.

Under the guidance of their Governor, Agricola, the Romans began to build a network of roads and forts, some of which led north from York. Many existing moorland tracks probably owe their birth to Agricola's plans. A Roman road was known as a '*stratum*' from which we get the word 'street', and the name still features in some villages around Malton like Barton-le-Street, Wharram-le-Street and Appleton-le-Street.

A Roman *stratum* was up to eighteen feet wide and paved with cobbles and large stones, with the centre raised to permit drainage into adjoining gutters. These roads were true marvels of engineering.

One 'street', a branch of Ermine Street, ran from Lincoln north to Malton and then through Barugh. In Barugh were some small camps, and the road continued to Pickering. From there it crossed the marshes of Ryedale and led into the Moors via Cawthorne, Stape, Goathland and Grosmont. There was a fort at Grosmont.

After Grosmont, it crossed the River Esk at a point which has never been determined, although portions have been found at Aislaby. It terminated on the coast close to Sandsend, a convenient landing point. Nearby is the Roman signalling station of Goldsborough and the village of Dunsley, which some writers claim to be the *Dunum Sinus* of the Roman period.

On the point of its entry into the Moors, some Roman camps were established at Cawthorne. Around AD 100 four Roman camps were constructed over two separate occupations. They lie almost due north of Pickering, on the summit of a five-hundred foot escarpment, and command impressive views all around. To the north the site overlooks the Moors around Cawthorne and the Victorian edifice of Keldy Castle, while the expansive Vale of Pickering lies to the south. There are several access routes, but the simplest is perhaps through Wrelton, where visitors should take the minor road north to Cawthorne village. The camps are positioned close together just north of the village on some rough moorland scrub, and at ground level they are not easily seen.

Excavations have produced few Roman artefacts, so it appears these were not permanent sites. Nonetheless, the searches have revealed objects like parts of chariot wheels, and fittings such as seats, which support the theory that these were temporary camps for troops on the march. They are thought to be the only remains of this type in the world.

The four camps straddle the route of the Roman road which ran north from Malton towards the North Yorkshire coast and form part of a network of Roman roads in this region; they are extremely well preserved. In 1983 the site was purchased by the North York Moors National Park Committee, and as I compile these notes, it has been announced that the site will be cleared of undergrowth and upgraded as a tourist attraction, with attendant car-parks and a picnic area.

By far the most exciting and best-preserved stretch of Roman road is on Wheeldale Moor, near Goathland, probably the finest example in Britain. It was placed in the care of the Department of the Environment, having been uncovered between 1914 and 1921. It lies to the north of Cropton Forest, six hundred feet above sea-level, parallel to Wheeldale Beck. It is part of the road which extended north-east from the Cawthorne Camps towards the River Esk near Grosmont. Access is either from Goathland or from the minor moorland road which runs from Stape to Egton Bridge; it is very close to Wheeldale Lodge Youth Hostel, and there is no charge for visiting this unique legacy of Roman Britain. It is sixteen feet wide and made up of flat stones laid on a bed of gravel. Raised in the centre to facilitate drainage, there are side gutters and culverts. The uncovered portion is about one mile and a quarter in length.

When we consider that it remained without any care or attention for centuries on a bleak and boggy moorland site, it is indeed a fine tribute to its builders. It is especially remarkable when we realize that only a century ago many of our present roads were little more than rough, unmade tracks. Understandably, it has suffered some damage, much of it by local people who used the readily available stone for their buildings, but perhaps it was the ever-expanding covering of heather which contributed to its remarkable survival.

Our superstitious forefathers knew nothing of its origins. In their eyes, it was the remains of a huge footpath which had been constructed by a giant, and it became inextricably linked with tales of the giant Wade from Mulgrave Castle. Legend said he built the road to help his wife, Bell, cross the moors to milk her cows. They had to traverse the twenty miles or so between the original Mulgrave Castle and Pickering Castle, a tough journey at the best of times. So Wade built this remarkable causeway for her. Such is the power and durability of legend that the road is still called Wade's Causeway, even though its Roman origins are not in doubt.

The Romans probably used oxen, horses and asses to transport themselves and their belongings across the Moors, and although their arrival and subsequent behaviour must have initially terrified the local people, they did stimulate progress and bring wealth, and their relationships with the residents became one of respect and even friendship. Moors people supplied the garrisons with food and equipment such as corn, meat and leather for their clothing and footwear. This trading was a necessary form of inter-communication, which led to the growth of many small villas.

A villa was a Roman farmstead, and several appeared around Malton and in the Howardian Hills. These were places of industry – there was quarrying, metal-working, farming, livestock breeding, pottery-making, arable work and, at Norton, even a goldsmith's shop managed by a slave. The villas themselves were impressive, with their heated rooms, baths, tessellated floors, painted walls, granaries and even horse- or donkey-mills. The local peasants probably worked here, but there is little evidence that the Saxons ever settled in these remarkable buildings.

Evidence of Roman presence has been found in Lastingham, Gillamoor, Castle Howard, Beadlam, Baxtons near Helmsley, Helmsley itself, Hovingham, Hood Grange, near the foot of Sutton Bank and in the name of the High Street above Ampleforth. The latter is about a mile out of the village and provides evidence of a Roman route across the hills; it is there that the beacon mentioned on pages 11, 16 and 100 is situated.

In 1612, at East Ness near Nunnington, a Roman sarcophagus was found. The inscription said, 'Valerius Vindicianus had [the tomb] made for his wife, Titia Pinta, aged thirty-eight, and his sons Valerius Adintor, aged twenty, and Varoilus, aged fifteen.' Interestingly, the area around Ness is known for its spring waters, which today serve the locality, and it is worth speculating that the Romans might have used this source and that these young men died protecting it from invaders.

The Romans appear to have influenced the Moors longer than other parts of the north-east, possibly due to their isolated nature, but in the early years of the fourth century they found themselves joining other moorland dwellers to defend their coastline from Saxon invaders.

The Romans built signal stations at strategic points along the coast from where they could maintain a watch over the sea and so defend their adopted country: at Huntcliffe near Saltburn, Goldsborough north of Whitby, The Peak at Ravenscar, and also Scarborough and Filey. Some of their remains can be seen today. These stations were linked to Malton, whose strategic location and proximity to York made it the ideal centre for Roman defences in the north.

The chain of coastal warning stations probably warned off many would-be attackers, but by the end of the fifth century the Roman occupation of Britain was almost over. The signal station at Goldsborough, for example, was attacked and its occupants killed. Excavations in 1919 revealed the bones of a thickset man with a dog at his side, its paws on his shoulders. Three skulls, some cloth, coins and animal bones were also found, and the site revealed a courtyard with six socket holes which had contained the upright supports of a roof. The signalling station at Scarborough, situated on land now within the grounds of the castle, survived a little longer, and further attacks from the north found the Romans in disarray.

As the fifth century passed into history, the Romans left the North York Moors. But history will never let us forget their presence or their immense contribution to the formation of the moorland character.

They left another legacy. Although they worshipped many of their own gods and adopted some of our heathen ones, they were responsible towards the latter end of their days of domination for the introduction of Christianity to Great Britain.

But this was soon to suffer, and the feeling of security generated by the Romans' long presence was severely shaken when the Moors were invaded by the tall, fair-haired Angles.

To their credit, they respected and encouraged family life and loved their homes. Each family lived in its own village, or 'ham', which was protected by an enclosure called a 'tun'. Many villages in the Moors and upon the surrounding plains remind us of their presence because their names end with 'ham' or 'ton'. Examples include Kilvington, Otterington, Stillington, Castleton, Hilton, Ayton, Stainton, Levisham, Lastingham and Yeddingham. Every householder owned his home and the land upon which it stood, while the ground around it was owned by the entire family. Beyond this, there were boundary markers, and unwary trespassers were likely to be killed by an arrow.

But the Angles were heathens who worshipped the sun, the moon and other gods. They included Woden, the spirit of movement, who showed himself in the winds and tides, Thor, the god of thunder, and Freya, the goddess of fruitfulness. We still remember these gods in the names of our days of the week, e.g. Wednesday, (Woden's Day), Thursday (Thor's Day) and Friday (Freya's Day). In addition, these handsome people believed in fairies, and one of their superstitions was to pass cattle through fire to protect them from evil spirits. I mention this because the custom was still practised in the north of England well into the last century. Old habits die hard.

The Angles were principally farmers who grew corn and bred cattle, and when they arrived in open rowing boats off our coast, they had to fight hard to occupy our land. But fight they did, and they rapidly occupied the North York Moors. The area between the River Humber and the Firth of Forth became the powerful Anglian kingdom of Northumbria. The North York Moors lay in the southern part of that kingdom, called Deira; the portion north of the Tees was called Bernicia. But the arrival of the Angles was not without conflict. This is reflected in the legend of King Arthur and his twelve Knights of the Round Table, who supposedly fought and defeated the Angles on Eston Nab.

It is without doubt that they did have a vicious and cruel streak. They killed the early Christian priests and burned their churches. Occasionally they married local women and kept their husbands as slaves.

One warlike ruler of Bernicia was Ethelfrith, who ruled between 593 and 617. When he attempted to conquer Deira, he caused its rightful heir, Edwin, to flee to East Anglia. Ethelfrith killed more than a thousand Christian monks in his rampage, and he scorned their faith by claiming their god had abandoned them. But even the mighty Ethelfrith was not immortal, and he died in 617.

This allowed Edwin's return, which marked another new beginning for the people of the Moors, for it brought about a revival of Christianity. Indeed, this period can be seen as the beginning of the local Christian era, from which the North York Moors have made a massive and lasting contribution to Christianity in England.

It began with an attempt on Edwin's life.

When he returned in 617, Edwin's strong rule over both halves of the kingdom of Northumbria brought a welcome peace. He defeated the Picts and the Scots, and even built Edwin's Borough, now Edinburgh. The new feeling of security led the people to say that, 'A woman and her babe might walk scatheless from sea to sea in Edwin's day.'

Though Edwin was not a Christian, this did not deter him, in 625, from marrying a Christian princess from Kent, called Ethelburga. He promised he would do nothing against the faith she professed, and when Ethelburga came north to begin her new life, a priest called Paulinus came with her. He tried to convert Edwin, but his efforts failed: Edwin prayed to his own gods while allowing Ethelburga to worship in the Christian fashion. Encouraged by Paulinus, later to be canonized as St Paulinus, she prayed that Edwin would be converted.

It was an incident in 626 on Fylingdales Moor, close to the subsequent site of the Ballistic Missile Warning Station, that changed his mind.

An assassin was sent by the king of the West Saxons to murder Edwin; he was to do so with a poisoned sword. Edwin's chief minister, a Christian called Lilla, was with the King at the time of the attempt. As the blow was struck, Lilla leapt between his King and the sword, and died instead of his sovereign.

Edwin was so impressed by the selfless devotion of his minister that he buried Lilla, along with some gold and silver artefacts, at the place which now bears his name, Lilla Howe. It also supports a famous stone memorial cross called Lilla Cross, one of our oldest Christian relics; it stands literally within the shadows of the twentieth-century Ballistic Missile Early Warning Station – a remarkable contrast between the ancient and the modern.

But that incident led to the foundation of Europe's most impressive church.

Edwin allowed his baby daughter and eleven members of his household to be baptized into the Church at Easter 626 and a year later adopted the same faith. He was baptized by Paulinus at York, on the eve of Easter 627. A small wooden church was used for the occasion, but Edwin decided to replace it with a fine stone one. It was the first of several on that site, the current one being York Minster, which was so dramatically damaged by fire in the summer of 1984.

Under Edwin, Christianity flourished throughout Northumbria. Evidence can be seen in dozens of ruined abbeys and hundreds of ancient churches scattered across the broad acres of North Yorkshire. Deep within the confines of the Moors, however, are some tiny churches which did so much to foster the faith more than thirteen hundred years ago.

3

Religion among the ruins

How like the image of repose it looks,
That ancient, holy and sequester'd pile.

Delta

Edwin's success led to a plot between Cadwallon, the Christian King of North Wales, and Penda, the heathen King of Mercia. They wanted rid of him and succeeded in killing him near Doncaster in 633. His body was buried at Streonshalh Abbey, although his severed head was interred in the Minster he had founded at York. Edwin's followers kept his faith alive by building little wooden churches around the Moors, while his death led to the appearance of his brother, Oswald.

But in 642 Penda also eliminated Oswald. The village of Oswaldkirk near Helmsley is named in his honour, and it is one of the few named after the patron saint of its parish church. The nearby Catholic church is named after Oswald's close friend St Aidan, who also played an important role in those turbulent times.

But there were more brothers to reign over the divided Northumbria. Oswy became King of Bernicia and Oswin reigned over Deira, the portion that contained the North York Moors.

Oswin was described as 'fair of face, tall of stature, courteous in manner and generous both to the nobles and to men of low stature'. He too was friend of St Aidan, but the saint feared that

'This king will not live long – I never saw so humble a prince and this people is not worthy to have such a ruler.' Oswy, on the other hand, was ruthless and ambitious. He wanted the whole of Northumbria – and the inevitable happened. The peaceful Oswin was killed at Gilling near Richmond by one of Oswy's officers, leaving Oswy King of Northumbria. Thus he ruled over the Moors, and he was a Christian.

To honour God for all his victories, including one over eighty-two-year-old Penda in 655, Oswy promised to build twelve monasteries and to make his daughter, Elfleda, a nun. She was sent to a monastery at Hartlepool whose abbess was his cousin, a princess called Hilda.

Oswy then began his monastic building programme – but even before his vital win over Penda there was a monastery in the Moors, at Lastingham. This remote but beautiful village in its exquisite moorland setting was described by the Venerable Bede as "among steep and solitary hills, where you would rather look for the hiding places of robbers or the lairs of wild animals than the abodes of man". Nonetheless, this tiny, isolated community became a noted centre of religious teaching and exerted a powerful influence upon English Christianity, especially in the north.

Founded in 654, the monastery at Lastingham was possibly the earliest in Yorkshire, but it should not be overlooked that Kirkdale Minster, only four miles away, was founded in the same year. This was less than sixty years after the Pope had sent St Augustine to Canterbury, and twenty-two years after Edwin's baptism by St Paulinus.

The story of Lastingham began when a monk at Lindisfarne, called Cedd, was given a piece of land at Laestingaen. He was there to found a monastery where the then King, Ethelwald, could hear the word of God, say his prayers and finally be buried. Helped by one of his brothers, Cynybill, and by a thegn called Ouini, Cedd began his task. He and Cynybill 'purified' their new site by fasting during Lent, after which they began their wooden monastery. Sadly, Cedd never finished his work. He went to the Synod of Whitby in 664 with thirty of his monks, but caught the plague and died at Lastingham the same year. At first he was buried in the open air, but later a stone church was built and he was interred to the right of its altar.

His fourth and youngest brother, Chad, succeeded him as Abbot of Lastingham, later becoming Bishop of York and then of Lichfield. It seems that the little monastery on the Moors flourished, to become an establishment of significance. With a stone church, it was operating when the Venerable Bede paid a visit in 731 while researching the lives of Cedd and Chad.

The brothers became two of our earliest saints, and their feast day is celebrated on 2 March. It is still marked by an old saying which dates to the time countryfolk kept geese: 'Before St Chad, every goose lays, whether good or bad."

Lastingham featured in 866, more than two hundred years after its foundation, when it was destroyed by the invading Danes, and another major event occurred two hundred years after that, in 1078, when Stephen, who was Abbot of Whitby Abbey, received permission from William the Conqueror to transfer himself and some monks from Whitby to Lastingham, with a view to re-establishing an abbey and a religious community. He did not finish, however, because he moved to York to found what became St Mary's Abbey, although he did build the remarkable crypt of Lastingham which can be seen today. If Stephen had finished his building, there would probably have been a ruined abbey in Lastingham now.

Almost certainly, the crypt stands on the site of Cedd's first monastery, and it is beneath the present church of St Mary. It is a unique early Norman crypt, one of the few apsidal crypts in this country and the only one complete with chancel, nave and two side aisles. It is a complete church in its own right. Now more than nine hundred years old, it probably stands over the grave of St Cedd and is therefore regarded as his shrine. It contains the remains of an ancient altar and some stone crosses dating variously to the time of the Angles, the Vikings and the Danes.

Apart from some plasterwork and levelling of the floor, the crypt has not been altered since 1088 – or, to make the date more significant, since William the Conqueror was in England. It is used occasionally for special services and is open to the public, access being through the parish church above. Since its early days, it has witnessed some odd events. One fiddle-playing vicar held dances here after his Sunday services, with food and beer as extras. He hoped to refresh and entertain the faithful who had come a long way, but the parties became so rowdy that he had to stop them. Cockfighting is said to have occurred in the crypt during the eighteenth century, and another tale says a lovely carved oak screen was broken up to make fuel for the smelting of lead.

In spite of Lastingham's stirring and noteworthy history, there is, from time to time, a suggestion that it is nearby Kirkdale Minster which is the site of that early monastery and the true burial place of St Cedd.

The first Kirkdale Minster was built around the same time as Lastingham, some four miles across the Moors. It is close to the noted Kirkdale Cave but its quiet location is so deep in the valley that it tends to be overlooked. It is a small church dedicated to St Gregory the Great, the first monk to become Pope, and is now used for Anglican parish services.

Kirkdale Minster is noted for an inscription carved in stone above the south doorway. This is a Saxon sundial, the most complete example of its kind in the world and bearing the longest known inscription from Anglo-Saxon times. It shows the eight hours of a Saxon day and was discovered beneath plaster in 1771. Replicas now exist in several museums, both at home and abroad, and as it was carved before William the Conqueror arrived, it is an intriguing reminder of life in Saxon times.

The inscription, translated into modern English, reads: 'Orm, the son of Gamal, bought St Gregory's Church when it was utterly broken and fallen, and caused it to be made anew from the ground, to Christ and St Gregory, in the days of King Edward and in the days of Earl Tosti. Hawarth wrought me and Brand the Priest.'

There is a lot of history behind this inscription. Gamal was murdered by Tosti, who was known as Tostig. Gamal's son Orm became a wealthy man and owned Crumbeclive, now known as Crunkley Gill near Lealholm, as well as land at the place known as Ormesby, near Middlesbrough. For his crime, Tostig was banished a year before the Battle of Hastings, and it was the same Tostig who was defeated at the Battle of Stamford Bridge by his brother, King Harold Godwinson of England, and who likewise killed King Harald Hardrada of Norway to give him the legendary seven feet of English soil.

St Gregory is Pope Gregory the Great, who sent St Augustine to England, an action prompted by the sight of some fair-haired youths exposed for sale as slaves in a Roman market. He learned they were Angles but called them angels.

The King Edward mentioned here is not Edward I of England, but one of the three Saxon kings of that name who reigned before Edward I. For this reason, some say that Edward I should have really been Edward IV.

It seems that Hawarth was the man who actually made the sundial, and the inscription enables us to calculate that the church was a ruin before 1066, the year when Earl Tostig was defeated at Stamford Bridge.

Another name on the sundial is that of Brand. He was thought to be the parish priest, for his role shows in the abbreviation 'prs' after his name, although one suggestion is that this means prior or even priests/priors in the plural. If he was a priest of that early church at the time, he is the first parish priest to be known by his name, and I sometimes wonder if this man also gave his name to the valley which runs down from the Moors and leads into Kirkdale. It is called Bransdale.

But is this intriguing old church the real monastery of St Cedd and also his burial place and shrine?

Two gravestones stand loose inside the church, having been recovered from the west wall; in living memory, one was said to bear an inscription to the memory of King Ethelwald, the man who asked Cedd to build a monastery, and this has led to speculation that the second was the tombstone of St Cedd himself. Is it feasible that the remains of the saint and his king were removed from Lastingham to Kirkdale in 866 for safe keeping when the Danes raided Lastingham? Or were parts of one old church commandeered to re-construct another?

It is interesting to ponder upon what could have happened all those years ago, and some visitors wonder how this tiny, remote church in Kirkdale comes to be classified as a minster. It is not the only local minster. A few miles away is Stonegrave Minster, a tiny parish church founded in 757. These small but lovely old parish churches qualify for this title because each was associated with a monastery where monks learned their faith and discipline. The term has not been applied to a church built after the Reformation.

As both the monastery at Lastingham and the minster at Kirkdale were under construction, Hilda, the Abbess of

Hartlepool, was transferred to Streonshalh. The year was 657 and this intelligent princess, later to become a famous saint, had already established herself as a woman of immense learning. With ten nuns, she travelled to Streonshalh, now known as Whitby, to establish a new monastery. But St Hilda did not occupy the building whose remains today stand so proudly upon Whitby's East Cliff. The original abbey was close to the site of the present ruin, but Hilda's was a wooden church dedicated to St Peter. It was built of rough tree trunks and thatched with straw and rushes. Throughout Hilda's reign it remained a wooden structure, only being replaced by an early stone building after her death on 17 November 680.

Hilda was called 'Mother' by the brethren, a sign of their affection, and due to her saintliness the local people knew her as 'Holy Hilda'. She was undoubtedly a superb abbess who ruled with a gentle firmness and who kept discipline among her inmates. Her clear-sightedness extended beyond the world of religion and touched upon the political life of the north-east. In 674 she became ill with fever but continued to work until her death six years later. Her powerful personality led to many legends: some believed she cut off the heads of all the snakes and turned their bodies into stone, a tale supported in primitive times by the ammonites found littered upon Whitby's beaches and cliffs and immortalized in Whitby's coat of arms.

Hilda's memory lives in parish churches named in her honour, and in village names like Hinderwell, once called Hildawell, and the vanished Hinderskelfe near Castle Howard. When Hilda died, her pupil Elfleda, the daughter of Oswy, succeeded her, and she continued to exert a powerful influence over Whitby Abbey.

Elfleda was a good friend of St Cuthbert and once sailed to Coquet Isle for discussion with him. She died in AD 713, and with her death ended the greatness of Whitby Abbey.

It is an awesome thought that the abbeys and monasteries of Lastingham, Kirkdale, Stonegrave and Whitby, with its cell at Hackness, made such an impact nearly five hundred years before the beginnings of the other great Yorkshire abbeys like Rievaulx, Fountains and Byland. The timescale is roughly the same as that between the births of our two Elizabethan Queens, Elizabeth I and Elizabeth II.

Two achievements by Whitby Abbey form part of our national history. One is the method of determining the date of Easter, and the other is the creation of English poetry through the work of Caedmon.

Arguments over the date of Easter go back almost to the Crucifixion itself, and it was not until AD 325 that the Council of Nicea decided that Easter would fall on the Sunday we observe to this day. But in England the people used their own. Celtic system of calculation. Oswy used this method, but his Queen, Eanfleda, used the Roman calculation which was favoured by Canterbury, and this meant that in England Easter was celebrated twice in one year! The task of settling the differences was allocated to a thirty-year-old priest called Wilfred, later St Wilfred of Ripon, but even this saintly man could not find a solution. The matter came to a head in AD 664, when Oswy called a synod to settle it. The site was the abbey of his cousin Hilda, at Whitby, then known as Streonshalh.

After considerable debate, the Synod decided that the Pope's system would be adopted for the whole of England, and so it remains to this day. Easter falls on the first Sunday after the first full moon that occurs on or after the spring equinox, which means that Easter may arrive on almost any date between 22 March and 25 April.

The Abbey's other achievement was to introduce the poet Caedmon to the world. He was a cowherd at the Abbey, advanced in years, untutored and religious. He was shy to the point of remaining in the background of the Abbey life, a facet of his character revealed by his attitude to the evening entertainments, known as '*gebeorscips*': when the fun required singing to one's own accompaniment on a harp which was being passed around, Caedmon would make an excuse to leave. He claimed the cows or horses needed attention.

On one such occasion, he disappeared but fell asleep in the stables. In a dream, a man came to him and said, "Come, Caedmon, sing a song to me."

Caedmon replied, "I cannot sing; that was the reason I left the *gebeorscip* and retired to the stable. I cannot sing."

The man in his dream said, "However, you shall sing."

"But what can I sing?" cried Caedmon.

"Sing of the beginning of created things," he was told, and, still in his dream, Caedmon began to sing to the praise of God. He used words and verses he had never previously known, and the words of his song were these:

Now must we praise the Warden of Heaven's realm,
The Creator's might and his mind's thought,
The glorious works of the Father; how of every wonder
He, The Lord Eternal, laid the foundation,
He shaped erst, for the sons of men,
Heaven as their roof, Holy Creator,
The middle world, He, mankind's Warden,
Eternal Lord, afterwards prepared,
The earth for men, Lord Almighty.

Upon waking, Caedmon recalled these words and could add similar ones. Concerned about his experience, he went to discuss it with the town reeve, who took him to see Hilda. When she heard his account, she assembled several wise men and asked Caedmon to explain his dream to them.

The little committee decided the gift had come from God. To test him, they produced some historical facts and asked him to turn them into a song. When he did so, they asked him to leave his work as a cowherd and join the monastery. Very quickly, he found himself turning the teachings of the Bible into verse and song. He sang of the Creation, of the origins of mankind, of Genesis, of the departure of the Israelites, of the Incarnation of Christ and many other things.

Dear old Caedmon was loved and respected by everyone; even teachers learned from his words, and it is said that Milton studied Caedmon's works before writing *Paradise Lost*. In 680 he died a happy and fulfilled man. (Hilda died the same year.) Caedmon is commemorated by a tall stone cross which stands at the top of Whitby's famous 199 steps. The cross is twenty feet high and fashioned in fine sandstone from Black Pasture Quarry, Northumberland. Before a huge crowd, it was unveiled on 21 September 1898 by the Poet Laureate, Alfred Austin, and it bears the words, 'To the Glory of God and in Memory of Caedmon, the Father of English Sacred Song. Fell asleep hard by, 680.'

Hilda founded other, smaller communities, such as a cell at Hinderwell, and noteworthy among them was one at Hackness, near Scarborough, which she founded in AD 680, just before her death; it was intended for her retirement, but she did not retire there.

One of the nuns had a dream which foretold Hilda's death. She was Begu or Bega, later known as St Bee, a nun for more than thirty years. She was woken by a bell, and when she opened her eyes, the roof was missing. A brilliant light shone into her room in which she saw a vision of St Hilda being carried up to Heaven by angels. When she was fully awake, Begu saw the other nuns were still asleep, and realized she had either had a dream or seen a vision. Sobbing, she ran to tell the Abbess that she thought Hilda had died. The Abbess, called Frigyth, summoned the others and they prayed all night. Next day, a travelling nun brought the news that Hilda had died during the night. As Whitby and Hackness are thirteen miles apart, there was no way Begu could have known at the time.

Hilda was sixty-six years old at her death, having spent her last thirty-three years as a nun, and her first thirty-three as a princess.

Nearly two hundred years later, that small establishment at Hackness was plundered by the Danes, two years after Whitby's abbey had suffered a similar fate.

After the Danes had destroyed what they could, the next two centuries witnessed very little religious influence or church building, and no monasteries were founded. Then came the awesome 'Harrying of the North' in 1069.

To crush those who might rise against him, William the Conqueror ordered this historic destruction of the north. He swore that he would not leave even the soul of the insurgents alive, and so his army set about its devastation of the north. One account said, 'It was not mere plunder, but simple, unmitigated havoc.' Houses were filled with corn, cattle and food before being burned to the ground. Cattle in the fields were slaughtered, implements smashed, houses and crops burned, and fields ravaged. North of the Humber, every scrap of food was destroyed, and there was not a single inhabited village between York and Durham. More than a hundred thousand people perished, bodies were left unburied, and plague or famine affected the few who survived. No ground was cultivated or tilled for years, and in 1135 a writer said, 'The ground for sixty miles or more is wholly uncultivated; the soil is bare even to the present time.'

The Moors were not spared. The value of land fell dramatically, and in the 120,000 acres of the Cleveland Hills, only eleven farmers were left. They had 225 villeins and labourers to operate fifty-eight ploughs. The coast, moors and plains suffered in similar manner. When the Domesday Book records this waste, it often uses the words '*hoc est wasta*'. Thirsk's value fell from £4 per annum to 10 shillings; Loftus was worth nothing, and twelve nearby villages were all waste, except Easington; Whitby and Sneaton fell from £112 to £3. From Crunkley near Lealholm to Westerdale, a distance of some eight miles in the Esk Valley, there was work only for eight ploughs, while Mulgrave and Hinderwell were waste. The Moors above Egton and Moorsholm were waste too, while Danby, Lealholm and Westerdale were worth 3 shillings, compared with £3 in King Edward's time. The Vale of Pickering also suffered. Pickering was worth £1.0s.4d instead of £88, Kirkbymoorside £5 instead of £12, and Helmsley 10 shillings instead of £1.12s.0d. Some six thousand acres around Ebberston, Snainton, Ellerburn and Thornton le Dale had only two ploughs instead of twenty-seven.

This wholesale destruction also caused suffering to the Church, as buildings were destroyed and lands laid to waste. When the Harrying was complete, William returned to York from Teesside and made a frightful winter journey down Bilsdale. But strangely, out of the destruction there came a fierce revival of religion. In the eleventh and twelfth centuries an increase in spiritual fervour led to the building of some new monasteries in the Moors, and the rebuilding of older ones. Some were of a very minor nature and have long since disappeared, but others became abbeys of importance and splendour. Many were to suffer again, when the Reformation laid them to waste upon the orders of Henry VIII.

Among the minor ones, William de Percy of Dunsley built a nunnery in 1133 at Handale near Loftus; around 1163 one was built at Yeddingham near Malton and dedicated to the Blessed Virgin Mary; then Peter de Hutton founded Arden Nunnery near

Hawnby in 1150. Later came the priory at Grosmont, founded around 1200 by Johanna, daughter of William Fossard. This was not linked to any English abbey but was supported by the French priory of Grandimont, or Grammont. However, Richard II allowed the prior to sell the advowson to an Englishman, and by 1394 the brethren were considered 'to be of the English nation', and it became known as Grosmont Priory. It vanished long ago. Two more were founded beyond the boundaries of the Moors, one near Richmond and another at Marrick, not far away. All were Benedictine foundations.

But the Moors contain two magnificent ruins of Yorkshire abbeys, Rievaulx and Byland, each founded nearly five hundred years after Whitby, Lastingham, Kirkdale, Stonegrave and Hackness.

Even in their ruined form, Rievaulx and Byland are magnificent. For sheer splendour they can match Whitby's lofty clifftop ruin. But these are not positioned high on a cliff for all to see; instead, they nestle in the deep folds of beautiful moorland valleys where their graceful walls rise from their lush surroundings to the delight of visitors.

Rievaulx Abbey, now with around a hundred thousand visitors per year, was the first Cistercian house founded in Yorkshire, and probably the most imposing. This largest of the Cistercian houses takes its name from the gentle River Rye, upon whose banks it stands. The nearby village bears the same name and is so beautiful that, in the words of a modern resident, 'A pub would be incompatible.'

Rievaulx is two miles out of Helmsley, and the pronunciation is 'Reevo', although the local people refer to the village and the abbey as 'Rivis' – indeed, some families living locally bear 'Rivis' as their surname. The village was honoured in the autumn of 1983 by Sir Harold Wilson, twice Labour prime minister, when, upon his elevation to the House of Lords, he became Lord Wilson of Rievaulx to commemorate ancestors who had lived in one of Rievaulx's lovely thatched cottages. The village was once known as one of two places in the Moors which contained a green telephone kiosk, but in recent years this has been re-painted red!

Rievaulx Abbey owes its origins to St Bernard of Clairvaux, who in 1128 sent some monks to contact a landowner in Helmsley, Walter L'Espec. Their efforts bore fruit because in

1131 he allocated to them 'a solitary place in Blakemoor near Helmsley surrounded by steep hills and covered by bogs and woods'. St Aelred said it provided 'a marvellous freedom from the tumult of the world', while William of Newburgh described it as a place of 'vast solitude and horror' ('*vastae solitudinis et horroris*') – indeed, wolves once roamed the valley. But after the abbey was built and later laid to ruin, writers invariably described it as one of the most beautiful sites and one of the most impressive ruins in England. Joseph Morris, in 1906, said it was 'the blending so perfect of ruined abbey and beautiful surroundings', and when Dorothy Wordsworth came here in 1801 she wrote, "I went down to look at the ruins. Thrushes were singing, cattle feeding among green-grown hillocks about the ruins. The hillocks were scattered over with grovelets of wild roses and other shrubs and covered with other wild flowers. I could have stayed in this solemn spot until evening, without a thought of moving, but William was waiting.' Walter Daniel, a monk of Rievaulx, said it 'provided the monks with a second paradise of wooded delight', and Arthur Mee, in his *King's England* series, said it was among the rarest treasures of our countryside.

The date of its foundation is variously given as 1131, 1132 or 1133, but the generally accepted date is the earliest of these, the date Walter L'Espec donated the site. Its first abbot was St William. Three years later, in 1134, Aelred, the man who became Rievaulx's most famous abbot and a saint, had a meeting with Walter L'Espec, from which we have a fine description of this generous Yorkshire nobleman. He was 'keen, wise and loyal, a staunch and generous friend, of gigantic stature with a voice like a trumpet, jet black hair and a long beard, a broad open brow and large, piercing keen dark eyes'. Another account says he was 'as large as a mountaine oake'.

Thanks to the impressive L'Espec's generosity, the monks were able to begin their colossal task – work which would take more than a century to complete. The geography of the site meant the church had to be built north-south instead of the usual east-west. The nave was probably finished around 1140, while the aisles of the chancel and triforium were not finished until 1240. During the initial stages, the monks lived in rough shelters, and the stone was obtained from two local quarries, then carried a mile or so to the site by barges upon the River Rye. Canals were dug to take the stone into the work area, and the Rye was dammed to flood the land near the abbey walls so that the stone could be floated as close as possible to where it was required.

As the abbey developed, so did trade in the area, and the huge church became a centre of activity, both religious and secular. It gave a much-needed boost to Helmsley as a trading centre, but even this busy town was overshadowed by the thriving abbey, whose interests included fishing, farming, sheep and woollen industry. New roads were built and workers flocked to this secluded valley; more and more land was donated by generous benefactors, and within fifty years of its foundation it possessed more than six thousand acres and over fourteen thousand sheep. Bilsdale, which adjoins Rievaulx, was then remote and undeveloped, and it benefited from Rievaulx's influence because new roads were built, bridges constructed and local people provided with employment. But the influence of Rievaulx spread far beyond the Moors.

Further Cistercian abbeys were built, with Rievaulx as their Mother Church; its abbot became head of the Cistercian Order in England. It was monks from Rievaulx, for example, who founded Melrose Abbey in Scotland, where the heart of Robert Bruce lies buried, and they also founded Revesby Abbey in Lincolnshire. As early as 1134 they turned down an offer of land from Olaf, King of the Isle of Man. They were too busy to accept it.

When Walter L'Espec retired in 1153, it is said he entered Rievaulx Abbey, where he later died. He was buried within the abbey on 15 March 1154, in front of the door of the Chapter House. Its first abbot, St William, and its most famous abbot, St Aelred, were also buried there.

Towards the time of the Dissolution of the Monasteries, Rievaulx was in decline, and indeed by the time of its dissolution it housed only twenty-two monks. At its height, some 640 men had been dependent upon the abbey, comprising 140 monks, 240 lay brothers and 260 hired workmen.

During the Dissolution, the abbey walls were razed in order to reach the lead on the roof, and the urgent work of the destroyers sent masonry and vaulting crashing down. Many of the houses in the village are built from those stones, but the lead from the roof was buried. It was re-discovered nearly four hundred years later and used in the restoration of the famous Five Sisters Window in York Minster. In April 1984 the preservation and control of Rievaulx Abbey passed from the Department of the Environment to the Historic Buildings and Monuments Commission, now known as English Heritage. Nearby Byland Abbey was also transferred to their care.

A few years after work started on Rievaulx Abbey, the abbot and twelve monks of Calder were driven from their abbey by the Scots. With their meagre belongings on a single cart drawn by eight slow-moving oxen, they trekked to the south. They hoped to shelter in Furness Abbey in the Lake District, but its monks refused to admit them. They turned towards the Pennines and Yorkshire friendliness, and were on the move for more than a year. Eventually they arrived at Thirsk.

There they came to the notice of Gundreda, mother of the noted landowner Roger de Mowbray. Locally, she was known as 'Gundreda the Bountiful', and when she saw the pathetic little group of poverty-stricken monks, she wept for them and promptly offered them shelter.

In 1138 she gave them a piece of land at Hood, which lies in the shelter of Sutton Bank, where her uncle, who had once been a monk at Whitby Abbey, was living as a hermit. Her son offered them shares in the supplies of Thirsk Castle, but as the distance made this impracticable, he gave them a cow pasture, and gradually they became self-sufficient. There was a setback when their abbot, Gerald, died in York, but he was succeeded by one of their own number called Roger. Under his guidance the little community thrived and in 1143, needing more space, they moved to the top of Sutton Bank. They had a new seven-hundred-acre site at Byland-on-the-Moor, also given by Roger de Mowbray, and a cell was constructed there, with a chapel at nearby Scawton.

But there was a problem: a massive new abbey was under construction almost under their feet in the valley below. This was Rievaulx. The problem was summed up by a writer who said, 'At every hour of the day and night, the one could hear the bells of the other. This was unseemly, and could not in any way long be borne.' Being men of religion, it was very unseemly to fight about it, so a diplomatic move was the answer. Once again, Roger de Mowbray came to their rescue, with a patch of land at Stocking, above Coxwold, and there they built a small church. For the next thirty years, this was their home.

But trouble struck again.

Their growing wealth and success caused some local landowners to harass them; they have been named as Robert Deyville of Kilburn, Hugh de Malbrise of Scawton and Guy de Boltby. As if this wasn't enough, the Abbot of Furness, a hundred miles away on the west coast, cast his eye upon their increasing wealth and decided he should have jurisdiction over them. He reminded them of the time they had left his abbey without seeking shelter and accused them of leaving his care without permission; they stated they had left because he would not allow them inside, so Abbot Aelred of Rievaulx was asked to settle the dispute. He ruled in favour of the tiny band of monks at Stocking, and so they continued with their independent community.

But they soon outgrew Stocking. On the Eve of All Saints, 31 October 1177, they moved into the broad valley between Coxwold and Wass. The ground was marshy but they could see its potential. The site was once described as being 'in the western part of the land of Cukwald [Coxwold] where they began manfully to root out the woods and by long and wide ditches to draw off the abundance of water from the marshes'.

Some early work was completed before they moved down from Stocking, and the present remains show that the builders always followed the original plan. The work was spread over many years, with contemporary buildings being erected to accommodate the working monks and helpers. The earliest work was in the south transept, around 1177, while the incredible west front, with its twenty-six-foot-diameter window, was finished in the thirteenth century.

Thus a magnificent new church was established on this wasteland, and it was called Byland Abbey. It is reputedly the largest Cistercian church in England, and its superb ruins are there to this day. They dominate and grace the valley in which they stand.

The sheer size of this abbey is staggering. Situated close to the road, a drive or a walk past the present ruins, imposing though they are, will fail to emphasize this aspect. The church portion is 330 feet long by 140 feet wide across the transepts, and the cloister is 145 feet square. By comparison, the cloisters at Fountains and Rievaulx are respectively 125 feet square and 140 feet square. The lay brothers' quarters, probably the first part of the abbey to be completed in stone, was 275 feet long and two storeys high.

The only way to appreciate Byland Abbey is to wander at leisure around its vast, empty ruins.

In spite of its size and majesty, Byland did not feature greatly in national affairs. One of its brushes with fame occurred in 1322, the year of the Battle of Byland, fought near the place now known as Scots Corner on the moors above Oldstead, not far from Sutton Bank top. (This should not be confused with Scotch Corner on the A1 trunk road in North Yorkshire.) At the time, Edward II was a guest at Byland Abbey, having returned from an unsuccessful invasion of Scotland. The Scots, led by Robert Bruce, surprised the English army who had camped on the moor nearby. They fought at Scots Corner, and the English army were well beaten. Edward fled from the abbey's protection, which was fortuitous, because the Scots then raided it, sacked it, stole his jewels and scattered the monks. He went on to York, and they raided nearby Rievaulx.

Due to the Reformation, Byland was suppressed in 1538, when its annual income was £295; at the time, its occupants were the abbot and twenty-five monks.

Many nearby buildings are constructed from the stones of the ruin, and today a semi-circular Norman archway from the abbey's gatehouse still spans the road to Oldstead. Motorists pass through it daily as they head into some of North Yorkshire's prettiest countryside, and the adjacent Abbey Inn stands on land which was once within the abbey boundaries.

There were several lesser Cistercian houses within the Moors. Keldholme Nunnery near Kirkbymoorside was founded in 1130 by Robert de Stuteville, and Rosedale Abbey was founded six years later by another man of the same nane. Wykeham Abbey dates to 1153, the work of Payn FitzOsbert, and at Hutton Low Cross near Guisborough a nunnery was founded in 1162 by Ralph de Neville – this was later moved to Thorpe, a small village which later became a suburb of Middlesbrough, known as

Nunthorpe in memory of those nuns. Around 1200 a nunnery was founded in Baysdale, a remote valley near Westerdale, but this and most of the others were very small establishments with about a dozen inmates. Few relics remain.

During this surge of building around the Moors by the Cistercians, the Augustinians were also constructing religious establishments in the area. The most important in the Moors, and indeed the most important in the whole of Yorkshire, was Guisborough Priory.

Founded by Robert de Brus, probably in 1119, it is tucked away beneath the northern slopes of the Moors, close to the centre of the town. Permission to build was given by Pope Calixtus II, and the priory was dedicated to the Blessed Virgin Mary. The first church was Norman and the second early English, but the latter was burned down due to the carelessness of a workman. While strengthening the roof, he was melting lead with a fire on the roof. He went away for a break and left his fire burning. The third church was built around 1309, and a member of the same Brus family gave it two thousand acres. At the time of the Dissolution, only Fountains, Selby and St Mary's Abbey in York were wealthier than Guisborough.

One legend associated with Guisborough Priory is that there used to be an underground passage from its grounds into an open area about a mile and a half away. Half way along was an enormous chest of gold guarded by a raven; the bird kept an eternal vigil on the treasure to prevent its being stolen. One day, however, a local man almost succeeded. He reached the treasure chest, and at that point the raven was transformed into the Devil. He promptly attacked the man, who managed to escape with his life. His adventure so terrified the local people that no one since has ever tried to find either the tunnel or the treasure. The tale was still told in Guisborough at the turn of the century.

Today Guisborough, a charming market town, lies in County Cleveland. An oddity which confuses outsiders is that the town is spelt 'Guisborough', while the family name of Lord Gisborough and Gisborough Moors above the town both omit the first letter 'u'.

The smaller Augustinian priories in or near the Moors included Marton-in-the-Forest near Brandsby, Newburgh near Coxwold, Kirkham near Malton and several to the west of the county in the Dales area. On the western edge of the Moors, however, are the ruins of the largest and best preserved of all the English Carthusian houses. This is at Mount Grace, close to Clack Lane Ends where the road from Northallerton to Osmotherley crosses the A19. Mount Grace was founded by Thomas Holland, Duke of Surrey and Earl of Kent, a nephew of Richard II.

This secluded priory remains of interest because it provides a vivid picture of the strict rule followed by the monks who lived there. Each had a two-storey cell, twenty-two feet square; the ground floor had a fireplace and a wooden staircase to the room above. Each cell had a small garden separated from the next by high walls. A door opened onto the cloister, but food was passed into the cell through a square hole in the thick wall, angled so that the inmate could not see who had brought it. The monks spent ten hours a day in their cells, reading, praying, eating and meditating, being allowed out only by permission of the prior. The full title of this gracious ruin is 'The House of the Assumption of the Blessed Virgin Mary and St Nicholas of Mount Grace in Ingleby'.

Nearby is the Chapel of Our Lady of Mount Grace, still used by Catholics as a place of pilgrimage. Mass has been said here for about six hundred years, and probably began when the first monks came to live here in 1398, while they built their priory on the plain below. The chapel suffered during the Dissolution, and there is a record in 1642 of its having no roof or shelter, only four bare walls. But that has been rectified, and at the time of writing the chapel is undergoing a massive restoration programme to cope with the increasing number of pilgrims and visitors.

Among the lesser religious houses was Malton Priory, a Carmelite house founded by Eustace Fitzjohn in 1150. Here the Carmelites became successful sheepfarmers, but their priory was plundered between 1243 and 1257 by Agnes de Vesci and some townspeople. The Carmelites also built at Scarborough and founded a house in Farndale in 1348.

The friars of the Holy Cross built a monastery in Kildale in 1312 but were asked to leave by Archbishop Greenfield of York because they had not sought his permission to conduct services. The Order of Knights Hospitallers (the Knights of St John of Jerusalem) also left their mark. In the reign of Henry II, they established a Hospitallers' Preceptory at Felixkirk near Thirsk, in addition to a house in the wilds of Westerdale. They were given land at Broughton, Kirkby-in-Cleveland, Wilton, Kirkdale and Staintondale. Roger de Mowbray was a benefactor to them – he seems to have emulated his mother in his acts of generosity towards religious people.

At Rosedale there is a short tower and twisting staircase, the probable remains of Rosedale Priory, a Cistercian nunnery built around 1158. It was dissolved in 1535 and occupied a site next door to the church at St Lawrence. Overlooking the site is a curious round sundial at the end of a small building; its appearance suggests it is of considerable age.

None of these religious establishments was destined to survive. The successful ones reached the height of their wealth about 1350, by which time many of the minor ones had already closed or disappeared, often due to inefficient organization. The major ones remained and continued to grow in stature and wealth until the middle of the sixteenth century, by which time a new danger threatened them because the Reformation was sweeping Europe. Catholic establishments were being destroyed or taken over by the Protestants, and so it was with our fine abbeys and distinctive churches. Even those within the seclusion of the Moors were located and ransacked. Around the 1530s, Henry VIII sent his commissioners into the country to lay waste the abbeys and churches. Those who refused to conform were persecuted, and many died for their ancient Catholic faith.

In the Moors, many abbeys ended their useful lives around 1536–9. They included Byland Abbey, Guisborough Priory, Malton Priory, Mount Grace Priory, Newburgh Priory, Rievaulx Abbey and Whitby Abbey, along with others far beyond the boundaries of the Moors. The ancient churches were taken over— and their wealth was ripped out as the new religion was statutorily imposed upon the people.

And so a great era was brought to a swift and savage end, but that old faith remained keenly alive in secret parts of the Moors. Many Catholics, especially priests, were executed during those 'Penal Times', but some avoided arrest by hiding in priest-holes which were skilfully and secretly constructed in the homes of both the well-to-do and the not so well-to-do supporters.

The Old Hall at Ugthorpe contained such a hiding-place in a

chimney, and this village, together with Egton Bridge and Grosmont in the valley below, became a centre of fierce resistance to the new state religion.

It was an Egton Bridge man who was largely responsible for keeping the Catholic faith alive on the Moors. Father Nicholas Postgate, now called 'Blessed Nicholas Postgate, Martyr of the Moors', was born in 1596 at Kirkdale House, Egton Bridge, and at the age of twenty-five went to Douai, in France, to be trained as a priest (this was illegal in England); he was ordained on 20 March 1628.

He was despatched to England as a missionary and arrived on 29 June 1630, probably landing in secret at Sandsend near Whitby, before heading for a safe house – there were several of these in and around Ugthorpe, Grosmont and Egton Bridge. He then spent his early priesthood as a chaplain to high-class families in various parts of Yorkshire, some of whom still survive. His true role was concealed because he worked as a gardener, gardening being one of his passions. He loved music too.

Postgate's desire was to return to his native Moors, which he did. He lived in a thatched cottage on a site still known as 'The Hermitage' near Ugthorpe, and travelled the length and breadth of the Moors on his faithful old horse. He always travelled in disguise and in secret in order to say Mass, distribute communion and visit the sick. To signal his impending arrival, a villager would spread sheets on the hillsides or along the hedgerows as if to dry. The number of sheets indicated the time and place of Mass.

On his travels he planted flowers, and tradition says he brought the wild daffodil to the Moors. He called it the Lenten Lily, and there was a period when pious tourists almost rendered them extinct around Egton Bridge and Ugthorpe.

Informers were a constant threat, so Postgate maintained his disguise as a jobbing gardener and used names like Watson, Readman and Roe, names of local families who still follow that ancient faith. And his fear of spies was justified. Following the panic generated by Titus Oates in his fake Popish Plot, an exciseman of Whitby called John Reeves (who had once worked for Oates) learned of Father Postgate's work and decided to trap him. For this information he would be paid £20, a huge amount in those times.

On 8 December 1678 Father Postgate was called to baptize a child at the home of Matthew Lyth at Red Barns Farm, Ugglebarnby, near Sleights. Assisted by a man called Henry Cockerall, Reeves raided the farm during the baptismal ceremony and found ample evidence that Postgate was a Roman Catholic priest. The aged priest was arrested and taken to Brompton near Scarborough, where he appeared before Sir William Cayley, the local justice of the peace. After hearing Reeves' evidence, Sir William committed Father Postgate to York Assizes, and he was taken immediately to York Castle, where he was imprisoned pending his trial. During his incarceration, he wrote a hymn entitled 'O Gracious God, O Saviour Sweet' which is still sung in Egton Bridge and elsewhere. Then he appeared before the Assize Court judge, charged with High Treason, and one of his own converts even gave evidence against him. He was found guilty; the penalty was that he should be hanged, drawn and quartered. He was then eighty-two years old.

On 7 August 1679 he suffered his punishment on the Knavesmire at York, on the site now occupied by the racecourse, and his quartered body was given to his friends. A copper plate was thrown into the coffin, and it bore this inscription: 'Here lies the body of that reverend and pious divine, Dr Nicholas Postgate, who was educated at the English College, Douay. And after he had laboured fifty years (to the admirable benefit and conversion of hundreds of souls) was at last advanced to the glorious crown of martyrdom at the City of York on the 7th August, 1679, having been a priest 51 years, aged 82.'

Although many relics of him and his work remain, especially in Egton Bridge, no one knows where his body was finally laid to rest, and that copper plate has never been found.

Up the hill towards Egton stands another memorial. It is the Mass House, a stone cottage with that name carved in stone upon its walls. It was here that Nicholas Postgate said some of his secret Masses and where, in 1830, a girl discovered a hidden loft with an altar laid out for Mass, complete with vestments, candlesticks and a crucifix. Later a hoard of silver coins was found hidden in the thatch, probably one of Father Postgate's last collections. Relics of his work can be seen at St Hedda's Catholic Church in Egton Bridge, where the Postgate Society is based.

For the record, Reeves appears to have been horrified at the outcome of his treachery, because he committed suicide by drowning himself in a deep pool at Littlebeck which has since been known as Devil's Dump. Rumour alleges that no fish has since been caught there.

The name of Nicholas Postgate remains alive in Egton Bridge, and on 31 May 1982 it was mentioned by Pope John Paul II, who, during the first-ever visit to England by a reigning Pope, stood on that place of execution at York and prayed a litany of northern saints. Among them were the great names of the area, including Hilda of Whitby, Cuthbert of Durham, Aelred of Rievaulx, Wilfred of Ripon, Cedd of Lastingham, John Fisher, who had served at Lythe, Aidan of Lindisfarne, Paulinus of York and others, such as Bede. And among them was the name of Nicholas Postgate.

At a very local level, he is remembered in a typically English way – the pub at Egton Bridge has changed its name from Station Hotel to the Postgate Inn.

Throughout the Moors' history, new abbeys have been born from the remains of the old, but it took nearly three hundred years for those old monastic traditions to be re-established in the North York Moors. Near Whitby is the Anglican Order of the Holy Paraclete at Sneaton Castle, and the two-nun monastery of the Assumption near Hawsker, a Greek Orthodox house. But by far the most impressive stands on the southern edge of the National Park. This is a modern abbey with a busy community of Benedictine monks.

Just as Helmsley and district used to depend upon Rievaulx's trading and farming expertise, so the same district, some eight hundred years later, benefits from the work generated by Ampleforth Abbey and its monks. The work of these monks involves teaching, for this is part of the Ampleforth College complex, England's premier Roman Catholic public school for boys. It has a world-wide reputation for learning and acts as a benevolent uncle to the surrounding villages. Several hundred local people work there. Hotels, inns, shops, transport, catering, local craftsmen, service industries and tradesmen all owe a part of their livelihood to the beautiful abbey which dominates Upper Ryedale. There are regular orchestral concerts and plays, and the Abbey encourages sporting participation by making its sports centre available to those who wish to join. Opened in 1975, it offers indoor swimming, gymnastics, tennis, cricket, football, volley ball, badminton, squash and other sports.

Its religious influence is felt world-wide too. Like Rievaulx in the past, its parishes extend across Britain from Abergavenny to the Lake District; just as Abbot Aelred of Rievaulx achieved eminence, so did Ampleforth's Abbot Basil Hume when he became the Cardinal Archbishop of Westminster. He played a major role in bringing a reigning Pope to England for the very first time.

The monks of Ampleforth belong to the Benedictine Order, and there is an unbroken line back to Westminster Abbey in London, long before the Reformation.

The abbey church was completed in 1961 and can be visited by the public. Visitors should descend into the crypts to see the twenty-five chapels, and upon request the abbot may appoint a monk to guide visitors around this remarkable place.

It all began in 1802, when some monks who had been exiled from France after the Revolution were given a house by Ann Fairfax of nearby Gilling Castle. (Gilling Castle, the stronghold of the Fairfaxes of Civil War fame, stands majestically across the valley and is used as a prep. school for Ampleforth College.) That house was on the outskirts of Ampleforth village and now forms the central portion of the growing school and monastery. The three monks who first occupied it began to teach boys in 1808, and within ten years the number had increased to forty-five. It is fair to say that the building has never stopped being extended, and as I write these notes, workmen have just completed a very modern Design Centre to teach crafts, computer skills and electronics; the old house which formed the early beginnings is being demolished and replaced, and the complex now includes a theatre, gymnasium, sports centre, spacious playing fields, library, TV studio and computerized library. There is also a music centre, refectory blocks, infirmary, indoor rifle range, three fishing lakes, a caravan site, a forest and more besides, including a farm and many houses. It hosts eminent people from all over the world, and on 26 June 1984 was visited by His Holiness the Dalai Lama, spiritual leader of the Tibetan Buddhists. I watched his robed figure walk among the black robes of our Benedictine monks.

St Benet's Chapel, in the crypt, contains the high altar stone from the ancient Byland Abbey, which is two miles along the road.

If one stands on the summit of Yearsley Bank, between Ampleforth and Brandsby, it is possible to see the ruins of Byland Abbey to the left and the modern bustling complex of Ampleforth Abbey to the right. Stonegrave Minster is further to the right.

These three churches so close together in one valley span more than twelve hundred years of religious history. It is almost as if the old have always given birth to the new, and that the work started centuries ago by the first monks of the Moors continues, and will continue, in the Moors.

4

Complements to the Scenery

> Progress, man's distinctive mark alone,
> Not God's, and not the beasts'.
>
> Robert Browning (1812–89)

The passage of time and the hand of nature have moulded the face of the Moors, while the ancient churches and abbeys have provided a rich spiritual and architectural foundation. But man has established other marks upon this landscape. For ancient defensive purposes he built castles and beacons, and for modern security he built the Ballistic Missile Early Warning Station at Fylingdales. For his journeys, he formed tracks and later built roads and railways. For his comfort and work, he built houses and farms, distinctive in their tough stone and rugged, practical style, and these were accompanied by forests, crops and reservoirs. There are bridges too, and memorials to men of note.

Man's artistry and his desire to imprint his presence on the Moors have emerged in prominent extraneous features like the White Horse of Kilburn and the abstract aluminium sculpture on East Moors near Helmsley. His broad sporting interests show in the tiny stone grouse butts on the lonely Moors, with quoit pitches and smooth green cricket fields in the dales.

The hesitant progress of mankind is therefore reflected in all these structures, and it can be said that the glory of the ancient churches and abbeys set the standard. None of the towns and villages can be described as ugly or lacking in style or interest, although it must be said that some of man's structures have led to a healthy controversy. At its inception, Fylingdales Early Warning Station caused an enormous fuss, yet many now regard it as an attractive asset to the district; similarly, Austin Wright's futuristic sculpture caused an outcry when it was positioned in glorious countryside, and yet it cannot be denied that it has character and charm.

But I begin with a look at the ancient castles. There might have been a similar outcry when these were built, because they were constructed on prime sites with outstanding views; they had to be large enough to house whole communities and stout enough to adopt the role of defensive bastions; I'm sure their aesthetics were never considered, but their purpose was never in doubt. Today we cherish our castles, and there are many around the Moors.

Around 1200 a survey revealed fourteen castles in the whole of Yorkshire, by far the largest concentration in any of the English counties. Of those, nine were in the North Riding, four in the West Riding, none in the East Riding and one in York. But this figure can be misleading, because in the course of history the Moors alone boasted many more than fourteen.

There is little doubt that the massive royal castle at Scarborough was the most important, with Malton, Pickering and Helmsley being secondary to it. But the others within the Moors or very close to them included the following: Sheriff Hutton, Gilling East, Cropton, Easby, Foss, Evers, Roxby, Danby, Crayke, two at Upsall, two at Mulgrave, two at Kirkbymoorside, Castleton, Felixkirk, Hood, Kildale, Kilton, Slingsby, Thirsk, Whorlton, Goathland, Ayton, Skelton, Ragby, Brompton and Kirkby Knowle. In addition, there are the recent Mulgrave Castle, Upsall Castle, Keldy Castle and Sneaton Castle, and the distinctive Castle Howard. There were more in other parts of the North Riding, such as Bolton, Middleham and Richmond, many of which played a significant part in national matters. Of those within the Moors, many have long since gone; those which remain provide an impressive reminder of past glories and stirring history.

Scarborough Castle, standing majestically beyond the boundaries of the National Park, occupies the site of a former Roman signalling station above the town known in Danish times as Skardaborg.

In 1136 William le Gros began to construct this massive defensive castle three hundred feet above sea-level. It is surrounded on three sides by the North Sea, while the fourth faces the town. Here William built a huge wall to make himself secure. The result was a castle which was almost impregnable, but this impregnability attracted those determined to disprove its invincibility. Some were successful.

It has featured in many national and local events. In fact, when Henry II worried about the dangerous power of his nobles, he ordered all castles to be demolished except this one. He realized that Scarborough Castle provided a strong defensive base, so instead of destroying it, he took it over. Thus it became a royal castle. He strengthened it, and it continued in Crown ownership to develop into a major fortress: in 1482 Richard III spent time here with Anne, his Queen.

During the Pilgrimage of Grace in 1536, Sir Robert Aske and some of his fanatics unsuccessfully besieged it, and in 1557 Thomas, the second son of Lord Stafford, and some of his conspirators managed to gain entry not by force but by subterfuge. Disguised as peasants and country folk, they entered Scarborough town on market day, and Stafford passed through the castle gates without any trouble. He pretended to be a sightseer, and in the same way thirty conspirators entered, to neutralize the guards and gain control of the gate. Then the rest of Stafford's men were admitted. In this easy, bloodless way, he gained possession of this supposedly impregnable castle, but it belonged to the King, and his success was very short-lived. Three days later the Earl of Westmorland regained possession for the King, Stafford and his men being swiftly executed in London.

It was this rapid retribution that led to the coining of the term 'a Scarborough warning'. The wording is, 'A Scarborough warning – a word and a blow, but the blow comes first!'

During the Civil War the castle was captured by Parliamentary forces. Sir Hugh Cholmley, who had deserted the cause of Parliament, was, in March 1642, commissioned to hold Scarborough Castle for the King, but it was unexpectedly raided by a Parliamentarian force led by Captain Brown Bushell. His element of surprise gave him success but not a drop of blood was shed. But Captain Bushell changed sides and admitted Sir Hugh Cholmley – so the castle was restored to the King. It had changed sides twice in one day.

But this was not the end. On 18 February 1643 the Parliamentarians raided the town and took it all – town and church, along with thirty-two cannons and 120 ships which lay in the harbour. But the castle was not taken and Sir Hugh Cholmley had managed to reach it, and there he remained. Led by Sir John Meldrum, the Parliamentarians attacked the castle, and their siege continued for more than a year until the occupants of the castle surrendered. They had no food, many of the soldiers had scurvy, some were too weak to stand up, and it is said that after the surrender the women of Scarborough threw stones at Cholmley for the damage his stubborn fight had done to the town. But the Royalists regained it, only to lose it again to the Parliamentarians in 1648.

In 1665, when Sir Jordan Crossland was governor, the castle held as a prisoner Mr George Fox, founder of the Society of Friends, or Quakers as they began to be known. He remained there a year, during which time he suffered from smoky fires, then no fires at all, and finally a room which let in the rain and wind. He was later freed to continue his work.

A few years before Fox's incarceration, an event had occurred which led to Scarborough's emergence as a noted spa.

In 1620 a Mrs Farrow, an intelligent and sensible lady, was walking along the shore when she noticed that some stones had become a rusty colour. Fresh water ran over them, and she tasted it, noticing that it was different from that of the other springs. For one thing it was more acid to the taste. She became convinced it possessed medicinal qualities and persuaded some friends to drink it. One old report says, 'It was found to be efficacious in some complaints and became the usual physic of the inhabitants. It was afterwards in great reputation with the citizens of York and the gentry of the country and at length was so generally recommended that several persons of quality came a great distance to drink it, preferring it to the Italian, French and German spaws.'

This was the beginning of Scarborough's fame as a watering place, and by the end of the last century it was the leading English spa town. Its qualities led to an influx of wealthy visitors, which in turn produced hotels, houses, a thriving port and eventually a railway and coach station. It became known as 'the Queen of Watering Places' and the pride of Victorian society. Today it remains an elegant town, a charming mixture of old and new, a gem of the Yorkshire coast. It is known for its wide south bay and sandy beaches, its holiday attractions, its art gallery and museum of natural history, the spa and its music. It houses the former summer home of the literary Sitwell family, the grave of Anne Brontë, the famous Theatre in the Round and England's most successful playwright, Alan Ayckbourn, whose plays are staged here before going on to London's West End theatres. Scarborough has enviable conference facilities and easy access to the vivid moors which surround it.

Inland is the market town of Pickering, which has an ancient castle tucked away almost out of sight. It seems difficult to locate but is worth the effort if only to inspect its deep well and the remains of its ovens.

The foundation date is not known but it probably dates from the early years of the Norman Conquest, when it was a timber fort. It has featured briefly in some national events – Richard II was imprisoned here before being taken to Pontefract, Henry IV and Richard III have stayed here, and Cromwell battered its stout walls with his cannons. One claim is that between 1100 and 1400 every English king came to hunt here and at nearby Blansby Park which was owned by the castle. The huge Forest of Pickering was a royal hunting ground, reaching from Rosedale to Eskdale and the coast. In addition, one of its towers, Rosamund's Tower, is said to be named after the Fair Rosamund Clifford, mistress of Henry II. It is not known why this tower bears her name because it was built a century after her death, consequently she could never have been imprisoned here as some accounts suggest. One theory is that she accompanied Henry on a visit to the castle, an event commemorated long afterwards by this tower's name.

Today, Pickering Castle is owned by HM The Queen through the Duchy of Lancaster.

Before the castle was taken into the care of the Department of the Environment, it was open to the public on Easter Day; tennis was played on the vast green lawns inside, and a fruit market was held within its walls.

The Cleveland Hills from Swainby Bank

Wade's Causeway, the Roman road on Wheeldale Moor

Above: Mauley Cross near Stape, named after the Mauley family who rebuilt the early Mulgrave Castle

Left: Caedmon's Cross and St Mary's Church, Whitby

Right: Lilla Cross, the earliest Christian relic on the North York Moors

Ampleforth Abbey from the south-west

Mount Grace Priory, a fine old Carthusian monastery near Osmotherley

Rievaulx Abbey, the earliest Cistercian house built in Yorkshire

The ruined east window of Guisborough Priory

St Gregory's Minster, Kirkdale, possibly founded by St Cedd in the seventh century

One of the Bridestones on Allerston High Moor. This and similar outcrops of rock have been curiously fashioned over the years by glaciers, wind and weather

Cropton Forest from a viewpoint near the Cawthorne Camps

One of the many grouse butts upon the Moors. These crude shelters are used by shooting parties as the grouse are driven overhead

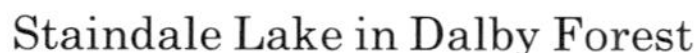
Staindale Lake in Dalby Forest

The Ballistic Missile Early Warning Station on Fylingdales Moor

Austin Wright's sculpture stands on East Moors, near Helmsley

But if the castle is difficult to find, then in some ways the town itself has an air of reticence. It is a peaceful, charming and even genteel place, thoroughly decent and nice. Near the castle are some delightful alleys and steps leading into the town centre, and in 1984 I found a pottery almost hidden from the bustle of the town.

In his book *Evolution of an English Town*, published in 1905, Gordon Home said it was difficult to find anyone in the south of England who was aware that Pickering existed. This view was reinforced on BBC Television in 1984 when a speaker admitted she had never heard of Pickering. It has carefully avoided national events and problems, but exist it does and, furthermore, it thrives. It is perched near the southern tip of the Moors, where it is appropriately known as 'Gateway to the Moors'. It lies just beyond the boundaries of the National Park but is full of interest.

The church should be visited, for its interior walls bear a gallery of fifteenth-century paintings; they were hidden by whitewash until 1851 when restoration uncovered them, but the vicar immediately concealed them again, after unsuccessfully trying to erase them. It seems he worried about idolatry! But they were uncovered again in 1878 and provide a wonderful welcome to everyone. They depict many events – there is St George slaying the dragon; St Christopher; Salome carrying the head of John the Baptist; the martyrdom of St Thomas à Becket and many more stirring portrayals.

Pickering is also a terminus of the delightful North York Moors Railway, which means that steam-engines hiss and whistle at the bottom of the busy market-place. The station hosts an amazingly well-stocked bookshop, while just along the road and line is a trout farm.

On the outskirts is the delightful aspect of Flamingo Park, a spacious zoo on a country estate, and the town also boasts an open-air market, the Beck Isle Museum of Rural Life, a clean selection of houses old and new, and a happy, robust atmosphere redolent of the moors which stretch away to the north. Between the seventeenth and nineteenth centuries, it was host to a thriving weaving industry, but this ended around 1850.

Pickering's shyness has resulted in its origins being uncertain. One historian, Stowe, believed the town dates from 270 BC, when it was founded by Pereduras, a king of the Britons. The town's name is said to come from an incident when he was bathing in the River Costa near the town, when he lost a ring and it was later recovered from the belly of a pike caught in the same river. According to legend, this gave us the name 'Pike-a-Ring', or Pickering. More probably, the name comes from the personal name Picer, the town being 'the settlement of Picer and his dependants'.

Higher in Ryedale, Kirkbymoorside's pair of castles have long since vanished. It is said that the stones of one were used to build the tollbooth in the market-place. But even without its castles, this small, very pleasant, stone-built town of red roofs and cobbled market-place justifies a halt and a gentle saunter through its peaceful streets. The church, which was being re-built when Wordsworth came by, is worth a visit.

The A170 sweeps past Kirkbymoorside, and because this carries away the bulk of heavy traffic, it does tend to isolate the town centre from passing tourist trade. This can be a mixed blessing: tourism attracts money and commerce but it also generates traffic problems, litter and other forms of human anti-social behaviour. It is one of the few towns without any yellow 'No Parking' lines on its streets.

If Kirkbymoorside has a claim to fame, it is because George Villiers, the notorious second Duke of Buckingham died here. There is a popular but false legend that he died in the worst room of the worst inn, but the truth is that he died in one of the best houses in Kirkbymoorside. It was occupied by one of his tenants and stood next door to the King's Head Inn. After a useless life of drinking, fighting and general misbehaviour, one story says Villiers fell from his horse while hunting in Bilsdale, and another that he caught a severe chill, but whatever happened, he was taken to Kirkbymoorside, where he died. His intestines were buried at Helmsley but his body was taken to London and interred beside his father's in the Henry VII Chapel in Westminster Abbey and not in the local church at Kirkbymoorside.

The town boasts an ancient legend that the Devil fought a witch at Yoadwath. The witch, known as a 'yoad' in old dialect, charged a fee to cross the nearby stream – such crossing places are called 'waths'. It seems that she and the Devil fought day and night over who had the right to the tolls. Sadly, I don't know who won!

Tucked into a lovely corner of Upper Ryedale, Helmsley is perhaps the busiest and most beautiful of its market towns. It may even be the most attractive in the whole of Yorkshire. Its position near the head of Ryedale, and on roads from Teesside and other parts of Yorkshire, makes it a natural halting place for visitors in cars and coaches. Everyone gravitates towards the charming market square with its monument to Lord Feversham, and the town attracts hikers who explore the Moors as well as those with less adventurous tendencies who simply want to stroll in peaceful surroundings.

Helmsley also has strong links with the disreputable Duke of Buckingham, and, indeed, one rumour said he died here and not at Kirkbymoorside. That he loved the town is not in dispute, for it became known as the 'the once proud Buckingham's delight'. It was a later Duke of Buckingham for whom Buckingham Palace was built in 1703, after which it was purchased by George III as a private residence.

The handsome houses and inns in Helmsley are built of local yellow stone, and most of them have the familiar red pantile roofs; even the council estate is built of stone. Most of the shops are conveniently situated around the market square. There is a purpose-built youth hostel and modern sports centre, while the summer of 1984 witnessed the opening of new restaurants and shops.

There is little doubt that tourism is demanding a response from Helmsley. And Helmsley is answering the challenge. There is an annual festival of arts and music and a newly opened centre for arts, drama and music in a former Quaker meeting house.

One forthcoming attraction is the opening of Duncombe Park to the public, probably in 1988. This fine country house stands in six hundred acres of parkland overlooking Helmsley, and in 1770 Arthur Young (who dismissed Castle Howard's landscape in a few words) wrote that he regarded Duncombe Park as 'the place in this country by far the most worth the attention of the curious traveller; it cannot be viewed without the most exquisite enjoyment.' The gardens may be open a year earlier, in 1987.

Duncombe Park Estate owns land in and around Helmsley, and with conservation of this beautiful building and its grounds in mind, the present Lord Feversham will open to the public his family house in Duncombe Park. Designed by Vanbrugh, it was proudly restored after a fire of 1839 and boasts thirty-five acres of gardens. Until its changed role, it will fulfil its present function as a private school for girls until expiration of the lease in March 1986. Then, after due modification, its doors will be opened to Helmsley's increasing number of visitors.

Duncombe Park will have to compete with nearby Castle Howard and Nunnington Hall, but its architectural merits, links with Bobby Shafto, fine views of Helmsley Castle and expansive parkland should generate the necessary acclaim. Bobby Shafto was the man who 'went to sea with silver buckles on his knee; when he comes back he'll marry me, bonny Bobby Shafto'. His links with the Duncombe family stem from his marriage to Lady Anne Duncombe, daughter of the Earl of Feversham. Bobby Shafto was, in fact, Admiral Lord Robert Shafto, who died in 1797 aged only thirty-six.

The Duncombe family purchased Helmsley Castle in the seventeenth century. It was built by Robert de Roos, Lord of Helmsley from 1186 until 1227. He was the son of Peter de Roos; Peter married the sister of Walter L'Espec, the founder of Rievaulx Abbey. Robert was sometimes known as Robert Furstan, and for this reason the castle was occasionally known as Furstan Castle. It belonged to the de Roos family until Henry VIII created Thomas Lord Roos, Earl of Rutland. Through marriage, it passed in 1682 to the Duke of Buckingham, and it was purchased in 1689 by Sir Charles Duncombe, a wealthy London banker. He died in 1711 and left the castle to his sister, Mary Browne, whose husband assumed the name of Duncombe. The Earls of Feversham, owners of the present Duncombe Park are descended from him.

The castle's only recorded siege occurred in 1644, when Sir Thomas Fairfax attacked it; the castle was held by Sir Jordan Crossland for the King, and he managed to sustain his defences for three months. But he surrendered on 22 November and the castle was then left in ruins. At the time, it was owned by the Duke of Buckingham, who later married Mary Fairfax, daughter of the man who had destroyed his castle.

The other surviving castles are deep within the Moors and are of a minor nature. Danby Castle was perhaps the earliest example of the palace fortress type in what used to be the North Riding of Yorkshire. It stands on the slope of the north-eastern tip of Danby Rigg, overlooking the valley of the River Esk, and it is not open to the public, although a prior letter might open its doors. It is now a farmhouse, with all the appearances of a fortified farm, and one of its rooms is used to this day for meetings of Danby Court Leet. As a child, its dungeon terrified me!

In its original role, it was the seat of the Latimers and claims that Catherine Parr, one of the wives of Henry VIII, once lived here. This is possible because she married John, Lord Latimer. The successors of this family, the Nevilles, later owned the castle, and its walls bear the shields of these families, and also of the Bruce and de Roos families.

Another interesting ruin not in the hands of the Department of the Environment is Whorlton Castle, near Swainby. There is no charge and no guide, but it is possible to enter this old building as it overlooks the broad expanse of land around Stokesley on the north-western edge of the Moors. Its past strategic position can be gauged by looking down upon the A172 and the surrounding villages, for it once surveyed all who came along that broad valley and its routes.

Whorlton Castle was probably built in the fourteenth century and once belonged to Henry VIII. He gave it to the Earl of Lennox who, by his wife (a niece of Henry's), was father of the Earl of Darnley, husband of Mary, Queen of Scots. It is said that the intrigues of that marriage were plotted at Whorlton Castle.

There is little here except the magnificent gatehouse bearing four shields carved in the stonework; they belong to three families, the Meynells, the Darcys and the Greys, and above them is a single shield impaling the Darcy and the Meynell families. Inside the gatehouse are the remains of the castle, scant as they are. In days gone by, it was surrounded by a moat with a drawbridge, and when I arrived for a look around, three workmen were cooking lunch over a log fire in one of its surviving twelfth-century vaults. The woodsmoke gave a curious sense of timelessness to the ancient castle.

Nearby is the fascinating and crumbling Norman Church of the Holy Cross, with a long avenue of ancient yews. Its history has run parallel with the castle, for its nave is roofless and the aisles have gone. But something of outstanding interest does remain. In addition to some Norman arches, there is a fifteenth-century tower complete with medieval bell, and a fifteenth-century east window in the chancel. This chancel remains roofed and is still used as a burial chapel, but it contains a curious stone cross propped up on a window ledge, and one of the earliest oaken effigies in England, a rarity anywhere. It lies upon a canopied tomb, probably dating to 1400, and is a hollow wooden figure in oak. It depicts a man lying with his legs crossed, and a dog at his feet, and it is thought to be that of Sir Nicholas, the second Lord Meynell, who died in 1322.

Whorlton was once a very important village, as shown by its lofty setting with a castle and church, but in 1428 its population fell to ten people due to plagues, and they moved down into nearby Swainby.

One fascinating aspect is the woodland on the slopes near Whorlton Castle. The trees have been planted so that, from the air, the initial letters E II R, in honour of Queen Elizabeth II, are picked out in the differing colours of the foliage.

Not all the castles are ruins. Upsall Castle near Thirsk was built in the last century on the site of a fourteenth-century one, and Gilling Castle, near Ampleforth, dates from the thirteenth century. The latter is still in use as a preparatory school for boys of Ampleforth College. Its magnificent Great Chamber, oak-panelled and dating from Elizabethan times, is used by the boys as their refectory. By courtesy of the Abbot of Ampleforth, Gilling Castle and its grounds are occasionally open to the public.

Another modern castle at Lythe is the home of the Marquis of Normanby, Lord Lieutenant for the County of North Yorkshire. This beautiful castle contains the stuff of legend. The original one was called Foss Castle, a timber and earth construction surrounded by a deep ditch. It was built by Nigel Fossard about the time of the Norman Conquest but did not survive. Another, more sturdy building, was erected on the site around 1190–1200, and this was in the ravined woods which surround the present castle. Those old ruins were pulled down in 1647, but remnants can still be seen.

The present castle, a lovely home in exquisite surroundings in the midst of gardens and woods, was built by the Duchess of

Buckingham around 1735. Dickens loved its gardens and views of the sea so much that he 'danced on the lawns in ecstasy'.

The early history of the castle is linked to a legend which has survived the passage of time, and which is still told by the people of the Moors. It is a fascinating mixture of fact and fiction.

According to the legend, one of the inhabitants of the early castle at Mulgrave was a giant Saxon king called Wada or Wade. He is said to be buried between two tall stones, one near Goldsborough and the other near East Barnby. These standing stones are about a mile apart, and each is known as Wade's Stone. The legend gave him an equally tall wife called Bell, and they built two castles, one at Pickering and the other at Mulgrave. As they worked, they tossed the hammer across the twenty miles or so of moorland between the two buildings.

But Bell kept a cow. To milk it, she had to tramp across the Moors, and so Wade decided to build a road for her, and she had to help with its construction. She carried the stones in her apron, and some fell out to form large mounds across the Moors. However, the road was finished and it was called Wade's Causeway. Some earth was needed during its construction and it is said that Wade scooped it out of the Moors with his bare hands: one resultant hollow is the Hole of Horcum, near Saltersgate. Afterwards, the spare earth was tossed across the Moors to form either Blakey Topping or Roseberry Topping.

The legend continued to relate that Bell was so huge that upon her death one of her ribs was retained. For a time it was kept at Mulgrave Castle, but it later proved to be a whale's jawbone!

Wade's road remains to this day, but we know it is really a Roman road. The truth can often spoil a good story.

If the Moors appear to be riddled with castles, abbeys and ancient churches to the exclusion of all else, this is not the case. Man has also placed vegetation around the Moors in the form of huge forests of coniferous trees.

Thick woodlands cover the hills and dales of the south-east corner of the Moors and give this portion a character which differs greatly from the remainder. Only something like a twelfth of the moorland area is afforested, but the rows of tall, straight trees provide a style and beauty of their very own. The south-east area is known as Allerston Forest and comprises several smaller forests, such as Cropton Forest, Wykeham Forest, Bickley

Forest, Dalby Forest, Langdale Forest, Wyddle Forest and Harwood Dale Forest.

Cropton Forest is some distance to the west, and Harwood Dale Forest lies to the north-east, with the others spread across the intermediate moors; there are more, smaller plantations about the Moors too, both in this locality and further afield.

It was in this forest, around Thornton le Dale, that the newly constituted Forestry Commission started its local programme of afforestation in 1920, only a year after the formation of the Commission. It has made use of marginal agricultural land and has steadily replaced older woodlands. Now, in addition to its thriving forests, there are some 35,000 acres of Forestry Commission plantations. Lots of these are on land either leased or purchased from private owners.

The Allerston Forest area is based at Pickering, while North Yorkshire's other forest area is based at Helmsley. This administers forests in the Hambleton Hills and Cleveland Hills and on the moors west of Rosedale. Between them there are more than 700,000 acres of afforested land.

The forests make use of the infertile soil of the upland regions, soil which will not produce sufficient nourishment for broad-leaved trees. The Forestry Commission has discovered that in the fertile valleys Sitka spruce and Norway spruce do well, but on the drier slopes the Japanese larch and hybrid larch are more successful. On the more exposed and elevated sites, the tougher pines, like the Scots Pine, tend to be used, while species from overseas have been considered. The importance of these trees is that they are grown as a crop, unlike famous forests like Epping and Sherwood which are mainly pleasure grounds. As a crop, they make full use of the land.

Although heavy afforestation of some areas has been criticized because of its detrimental effect upon wildlife, it is proving vital to the economy of the area. The forests provide hundreds of jobs and make use of land which would otherwise be unproductive. Many woodmen live in forest villages specially constructed for them at Low Dalby, Wykeham Moor and Darncombe. There are also some remote and scattered forest homes, frequently with an adjoining patch of land for cultivation by the occupiers. Low Dalby caters for the visitor with its Forestry Information Centre, which explains forestry work and provides a marvellous guide to the wildlife of the area. Generally speaking, the forests are open to the public, with adequate car-parks, picnic areas, forest drives and vantage points along miles of forest track. The Commission genuinely welcomes visitors and provides holiday cabins for rent but asks that great care be taken to avoid the risk of fire. A carelessly thrown cigarette or match can destroy the work of many years, and there is no doubt the forestry workers are extremely proud of their forests.

But if the forests have produced their own villages, there are also some older communities within them, communities that have been there for centuries. One of the most attractive is Hackness, near Scarborough. It is one of the most beautiful villages in Yorkshire, described as 'sweetly placed by the river', and lies deep in the lovely valley of the Derwent. The houses are constructed in a mellow stone which gives the village a sense of history and peace. Few villages have a more pleasant setting, for there are many streams, one of which flows in an artificial bed beside the road, together with the moors, forests and fine views all around. Above, the heights provide ranging views of the coastline and North Sea and thrilling drives along lanes of tall trees. The River Derwent accepts the waters of many becks which flow down through the forests, and some valleys are so deep and steep that one farm near Cochrah is said never to see the sun between October and March.

The small valleys which run into Hackness Vale were described by the poet William Mason as

> A nest of sister vales, o'er hung with hills,
> Of varied form and foliage.

A monastery was founded at Hackness in 680, and the present Church of St Peter at Hackness, with its heavy oak pews, was started in Saxon times, around 1050, almost a century before Scarborough Castle, and was then a Benedictine monastery. It has a thirteenth-century tower with a fifteenth-century spire on top. The font has a magnificent tall oak cover carved in 1480, with eight figures in pearwood added later, having been carved in Oberammergau. Another unique sight is a Saxon cross which commemorates one of the abbesses of Hackness and was probably made around 720. It bears Latin and Saxon inscriptions.

Hackness is known as the birthplace of the sculptor Matthew Noble, who carved famous statues including that of the Earl of Derby in London's Westminster Square, Sir John Franklin in Waterloo Place and Sir James Outram on the Embankment. He exhibited more than a hundred works in the Royal Academy and is buried at nearby Brompton.

Downstream is Everley, a hamlet which marks the start of the remarkable Derwent Sea Cut. This slices across the landscape like a neat canal, for it is a man-made waterway.

The Derwent, with its huge volume of winter catchment water, used to flood massive areas of the Vale of Pickering, including the towns of Malton and Pickering, but Sir George Cayley of Brompton came up with a remarkable solution. Between 1800 and 1810 a channel was cut by hand from Everley to the North Sea at Scalby Mills. A sluice allows the normal waters of the Derwent to follow the course of the river, but any excess flows over the sluice and into the Cut, from where it heads for the safety of the North Sea, some five miles away.

From Hackness Vale, the beautiful Forge Valley carries a road and a long-distance footpath called the Derwent Way into Ayton. Between them, Hackness Vale and Forge Valley, a National Nature Reserve, provide some of the most impressive scenery around Scarborough.

At West Ayton are the meagre remains of a castle owned by the Evers family, after whom Everley appears to be named, although one source of the village name does suggest a 'wild boar clearing'.

Forge Valley, noted for its profusion of ash trees, is said to have got its name because some monks of Rievaulx established an iron forge at its northern end, and indeed there was a foundry here in 1798, although now it would be difficult to find remains. This is a valley of densely growing deciduous trees, such a change from the conifers of the surrounding hills.

Nearby are two of the more pleasantly named dales of the Moors, Troutsdale and Whisperdale, whose waters pour into the Derwent. A winding, narrow road runs through lovely Troutsdale, but Whisperdale should be approached on foot. Its delightful name comes from White Spot Valley, hinting at far-off links between Whitby Abbey and Hackness.

Troutsdale can be reached from Snainton, and the scenic road runs near Cockmoor Hall, some seven hundred feet above sea-level. At this point there is a car-park with breathtaking views over Troutsdale, and close by are some magnificent multiple earthworks about a quarter of a mile from the Hall. These are known as Cockmoor Dykes, said to be the finest in Yorkshire, while Scamridge Dykes and Givendale Dykes also mark this stretch of low-lying moor.

In addition to the foregoing man-made additions to the landscape of the Moors are hundreds of curious standing stones or crosses. The entire collection forms what is probably Britain's largest assembly of standing stones, certainly the largest assembly in such a compact area, and they include parish boundary markers, the remains of stone circles, earthworks, way markers, religious crosses and memorials.

For example, on a map of Glaisdale produced after a survey between 1849 and 1853, I found Yoak stones, grey stones, the Rokan Stone, Hart Leap Stones and dozens of others marked simply 'stone' or 'stones'. One collection is marked on the map as 'pile of stones'. Significantly, many are shown along the routes of ancient tracks – for example, running from Ainthorpe to Fryup over Danby Rigg was the Old Wife's Stones Road, now a footpath, and it's feasible that the Rokan Stone was a marker on an old route or a boundary marker. I wondered also if it was to guide wayfarers in fog – the dialect word for a fog on those moors is 'roak' or 'roke'.

The similarly named Yoak stone comes from 'ye olde oak tree stone', a parish boundary marker of bygone days, while the Hart Leap stones mark the terrified leap of a hunted deer which leapt fourteen yards to its freedom.

Some of the Moors' stones are perfect examples of medieval craftsmanship, while others are little more than deserted bases or merely sites of former crosses. Some are nothing more than natural outcrops of rock jutting from the moorland, sculpted to the form of tall stones by the fierce weather.

Crosses or stones also mark significant events, such as the discoveries of Captain Cook or the more local life of Frank Elgee. The Elgee Memorial Stone is a flat-topped boulder overlooking Loose Howe on Rosedale Moor. It reminds us of the life and writings of the 'man of the Moors', Frank Elgee, naturalist, archaeologist and author of the classic book *The Moorlands of North East Yorkshire*, published in 1912. The boulder which bears his name gives his date of birth (1880) and the date of his death (1944) and says that it was unveiled by his widow in 1955.

But there are stones of great antiquity too. Lilla Cross on Fylingdales Moor, mentioned in page 34, dates to AD 626, and one of indeterminate age is the cross erroneously known as Ralph's Cross. This is featured on the logo of the North York Moors National Park.

As a boy, I would cycle from Glaisdale via Castleton to the windswept heights of Danby High Moor. Close to the lofty meeting-place of roads leading to Westerdale, Hutton-le-Hole, Rosedale and Castleton, stands this distinctive waymarker, correctly known as Young Ralph. It should not be called Ralph's Cross. Other nearby stones include Fat Betty, Old Ralph and the Elgee Memorial Stone, but as a child my purpose was to find out whether anyone had left money in the hollow at the top of the nine-foot-tall Young Ralph. It meant propping my cycle precariously against the stem and standing on the saddle to reach the hollow. Sometimes I would be rewarded with a threepenny bit, for it has long been customary for passers-by to put money there for weary travellers. I defended my action by classifying myself as a weary traveller, which for a boy of ten or eleven was true, but in later years I repaid my alms by placing more money there. When we called in the spring of 1984, Young Ralph contained several 2p pieces, and to keep the custom alive my son placed his donation in the shallow hollow on top.

It was this custom which almost destroyed Young Ralph. In 1961 the slender stem broke as a man tried to recover some coins, and today the careful repairs bear testimony to that unfortunate episode in Young Ralph's history. A pointless attack occurred in October 1984 when the cross was vandalized by having a rope tied around it and then being dragged from its base by a vehicle. It fell to the ground and suffered some damage, but happily it was not beyond repair.

But what is the purpose of Young Ralph, and why is this cross located on this lonely moor top? Legend says that an eighteenth-century traveller died through exhaustion and that a local farmer called Ralph arranged for the erection of this tall stone cross on the site. He ordered a hollow to be fashioned in the top so that those who could afford it would place funds there for the benefit of less fortunate travellers. Its age is unknown, but the present cross is thought to be an eighteenth-century replica of the original highway marker.

Old Ralph, only five feet high, stands on the moor a couple of hundred yards away to the south-west, while along the road to Rosedale is the bulky, white-painted form of Fat Betty, or the White Cross as it is formally known. This is not a cross but a solid lump of rock, one of several on the Moors which bear a personal name. Other named crosses include the Margery Stone (which is nearby), the Percy Cross, Jack Cross, John Cross, John o' Man, Cooper Cross, Tom Smith's Cross, Donna Cross, Jenny Bradley, Redman Cross, Anna Ain Howe Cross, Robinson's Cross and Hudson's Cross. One complete example of an ancient stone cross is Mauley Cross, named after the de Mauleys of Mulgrave Castle. It stands just inside Cropton Forest, at the side of the forest track which emerges near Stape. There are three Job Crosses on the Moors, probably boundary markers. The real reason for all these names is not easy to determine. Invariably, there are stories and legends linked to them, some of which have been forgotten.

According to Ampleforth people, for example, Tom Smith's Cross, above their village at the side of the A170, commemorates the gibbeting of a highwayman. The cross was recorded as a standing stone in 1642 but is no longer there. The location is now a crossroads leading into Ampleforth, Wass and Oswaldkirk from the main road and is not shown on modern maps by that name.

But of all the stones upon the Moors, it is perhaps Fat Betty and her proximity to the two Ralphs which has attracted the most durable stories. Like so many of the Moors tales, they are liberally spiced with a mixture of fact and fiction.

One story tells of a party of nuns travelling from York to Baysdale Abbey near Westerdale. They became separated in thick fog and, fearing for their lives on those bleak moors, began to call out to one another. They were soon re-united, only to discover that they had not strayed very far. To commemorate their deliverance, it is said they erected a cross – Fat Betty – on the place where they were re-united.

Another tale links Fat Betty with Old Ralph. Some Cistercian nuns, known as the White Ladies, had established a nunnery in Rosedale. Their arrival aroused a good deal of suspicion and even antagonism among the local people but an old man called Ralph became their devoted servant. One of his duties was to guide them upon their moorland missions.

When a question of religious interpretation arose, one of the nuns, Sister Elizabeth, had to meet a representative of Baysdale Abbey to iron out the problem. The meeting was arranged at a stone cross on the Moors, midway between the two communities. Old Ralph therefore escorted Sister Elizabeth to this isolated place, but no one arrived. Ralph and Elizabeth waited for a long time, and then Ralph decided to set off to find the missing Baysdale nun, called Margery. A thick mist or roak developed, and Ralph maintained contact with Sister Elizabeth by shouting, but could not locate Margery. Then the fog lifted, and all three found themselves very close together, Sister Margery having remained motionless, too terrified to respond to the shouting of an unknown man.

Old Ralph is said to have marked the occasion by positioning these standing stones. The Margery Stone, sometimes called Old Margery, still acts as a way marker for hikers on the Lyke Wake Walk and is a rendezvous point for support parties. The other members of her original party continue to stand in silence at a discreet distance.

It is felt, by the way, that the name Fat Betty relates to the size of the white boulder and not to the measurements of Sister Elizabeth! And there is a further tradition that if ever Old Ralph and Fat Betty meet, they will be married.

There are too many of these stones to list here, but a curious one is the Face Stone, mentioned in a perambulation of the Helmsley Estate boundaries in 1642. Its unique feature is the face carved upon it, and it is not known whether it marks a grave or whether a passer-by with time on his hands managed to carve this face.

Such is the fascination of all these remarkable and varied stones that a long-distance walk has been established to tour some of them. In October 1971 the fifty-three-mile Crosses Walk was inaugurated and encompasses just over a dozen crosses and stones. It is a tough walk and not for the inexperienced or ill-equipped.

Carved stones and crosses can also be found in our moorland churches, many marking the return of Christianity, and Ryedale churches are particularly rich with them. They can be seen at

Hovingham, Stonegrave Minster, Oswaldkirk, Middleton, Kirkdale Minster, Lastingham, Nunnington, Hawnby and others.

Other standing stones include the Bridestones, and the Moors contain several groups known by this name. The group near Staindale appears to be a natural feature, while a circle on Nab Ridge above Bilsdale is probably the remains of an ancient burial ground. Another ring stands on the aptly named Standing Stone Rigg near Harwood Dale, and this once surrounded a barrow in which there was a smaller stone burial chamber dating to the early Bronze Age.

On the edge of the escarpment to the east of Carlton-in-Cleveland is a collection of stones known as the Wainstones, an ancient natural feature whose name is used locally as the telephone exchange for the locality, a popular rock-climbing venue. It is suggested the name comes from the Saxon word 'wanian' meaning 'to howl', a reference to the noise of the wind as it whirls about this lofty, isolated region. It could also be linked to Whinstone, a volcanic rock locally called blueflint or bluestone. This was once regarded as the best road material quarried in the north, and some moorland grave mounds were fashioned from this rock, mined from Whinstone Dyke. One belief is that the Wainstones were stones of lamentation.

Near Carlton Bank Top is a marker stone known as Three Lords Stone; it is 975 feet above sea-level and marked the meeting-point of three lords' estates – Duncombe of Helmsley, Marwood of Busby Hall and Aylesbury of Snilesworth.

Also dominant on the Cleveland Hills at the western edge of the Moors is the Cook Monument on Easby Moor above Great Ayton. It was erected in 1827 to the memory of the great navigator and discoverer of Australia and is an obelisk more than fifty feet tall which is visible from a considerable distance.

It was on the edge of the Moors near Great Ayton that Captain Cook's father obtained work at Airyholme Farm, which is still on the southern slopes of Roseberry Topping. Cook himself worked on the farm for about two years.

James Cook was born in 1728 at Marton near Middlesbrough and was eight when his family moved to Great Ayton. His school is now a small museum, and his parents retired to a cottage in the village, the family graves occupying space in the churchyard.

In 1934 that cottage was moved stone by stone and re-erected in Melbourne, Australia.

Many of the stones and monuments can be visited with comparative ease but others require a long, arduous trek across rough, open moorland.

Two of the most prominent Moors landmarks are surely Fylingdales Ballistic Missile Early Warning Station, with its radomes, and the White Horse of Kilburn. Each is visible from a long distance, each is coloured white which is outstanding against the earthy shades of the moorland, and each provides a landmark for people both on the ground and in the air.

The Early Warning Station can be compared with the ancient beacons of Roman times, the castles of medieval times and even Danby Beacon, which, during World War II, served as an RAF radar station. Their defensive roles are so similar – each stands or stood upon a lofty site to protect the people, and in Fylingdales' case, not only the people of the moors but the whole of Western free society.

I can remember the growing shape of the three white radomes, like huge eggs or golf balls, as they materialized upon our Moors in the early 1960s. In some lights they appear to be a delicate shade of duck-egg blue while at other times they are mottled. Without question, they do possess an unusual beauty, but the buildings which surround them fail to enhance the scenery in any way. It is the three white balls which dominate the landscape, and although there were protests against the construction of this station, some based upon its aesthetics, it is now a major attraction and people happily picnic in nearby Ellerbeck beneath its shadows.

There is a curious anomaly because this futuristic equipment stands almost next to one of the most ancient things of interest on the Moor, Lilla Cross, and it surpasses the role of the early beacons and even the radar of RAF Danby Beacon.

So what is the function of these three giant golf balls? Each of the radomes is more than fifty yards high and houses radar dishes which swivel as they monitor the airspace up to three thousand miles away. They are capable of detecting objects as small as footballs over Moscow and form a worldwide link with similar stations in Greenland and Alaska. They can observe and monitor missiles in space too, and the station is involved in space missions; it also monitors space for satellites and other circulating objects. Its purpose, when opened in 1964, was to provide the free world with four minutes warning of the launch of a nuclear attack upon this country. Although much of its value lies in its deterrent role, this warning is not as silly or as pointless as some would lead us to believe. Before a war begins, there are the inevitable months of tension, the weeks of diplomatic activity and the bleak final days before war is declared. The probability of a nuclear attack would be known hours, weeks or even months in advance; that four-minute warning tells us what we have feared all the time and gives us time to act upon our prepared plans – if we haven't already done so.

If the siting of Fylingdales was justified because of its necessary role, one wonders if there was any outcry when Mr John Hodgson, the village schoolmaster at Kilburn, decided to carve a massive white horse upon the hillside above that lovely village. He drew his plans in October 1857 and, with the help of his pupils, produced an outline of the proposed horse. Thirty-three local men were recruited to carve it from the hillside, and it was completed in November 1857, the only one of its kind in the north of England.

It is almost 105 yards long by some seventy-six yards high; two dozen people can sit on the circle of grass which forms its eye, and when it was originally cut from the earth, more than six tons of lime were required to whiten it. Unlike the more ancient white horses which are carved from the landscape, the Kilburn Horse is not cut from chalk but has a limestone base which is a dullish brown colour. For this reason, it has to be kept regularly topped up with white materials. Furthermore, the outline tends to disintegrate due to the weather, the natural erosion of the land and thoughtless visitors who walk upon it; consequently upkeep of the horse is a major headache. But the people of Kilburn, and indeed the whole of Yorkshire, are proud of their White Horse, and there is now a registered charity to ensure it is kept neatly groomed. To persuade visitors to climb the steep hill and view it correctly, a flight of steps has been installed.

The horse can be seen up to seventy miles away, and for any North Yorkshire person returning from the south by road, rail or air, this is one of the signs that they are within reach of home.

Perhaps the problems of upkeep of the horse can be summed up by the words of Mousey Thompson himself, the famous woodcarver of Kilburn. Someone suggested it was an easy matter to whitewash the horse, and he retorted, 'Has thoo ever tried whitewashing a ploughed field?'

Whether or not Mr Hodgson faced opposition to his idea, a sculptor who was commissioned to erect a work upon the Moors did face severe criticism. In September 1977 an aluminium sculpture was erected on an escarpment at Roppa Bank, some four miles north of Helmsley. Commissioned by the Yorkshire Arts Association, and narrowly approved by the North York Moors National Park authority, it was the work of the York sculptor Austin Wright. It comprises two large irregular rings of aluminium, each about eight feet high, which stand close together in their concrete base. Critics said the two giant rings were like bicycle wheels picked up at a scrapyard, but in the time since the sculpture was set in position, there have been few complaints. Indeed, many visitors enjoy their picnics nearby and observe the changing and extensive moorland scenes through these curious rings. My own view is that it is no more out of place than any other structure on the Moors, and I find it quite dramatic and interesting.

This and Fylingdales bring the Moors into the twentieth century.

5

Upon the Solitary Hills

'The Moor is of an open and free nature.'
William Shakespeare (1564–1616)

It is the central upland portion which gives the North York Moors character and reputation. This is the area where the grouse fly free and the heather grows purple and strong, where hardy sheep graze without restriction as they have in centuries past, where peat is still cut for fires and where the wind blows strong with the scent of the sea. Ferocious winters can bring life to a standstill while the heat of summer makes the moorland shimmer and bake.

Writers have variously described these moors as forbidding, barren, awesome, bleak, windswept, isolated, lonely and sometimes beautiful, dramatic or picturesque. They are all that – and more, and it is the duty of the North York Moors National Park Commitee to ensure that the area remains unspoilt.

The moorfolk themselves will pretend there is little worth coming to see or to experience, and they have often persuaded outsiders that their beautiful and beloved landscape compares with the industrial wastes of West Yorkshire or South Yorkshire, or that its villages conform to the image of an industrial area. I will accept the claims of beauty, but comparisons with industrial murk and grime could not be further from the truth. But the moorfolk have succeeded in maintaining their homeland as one of the great unexplored and exploited regions of England. It is a matter of some pride and amusement among them that they have persuaded would-be visitors to keep away, but this last of Yorkshire's secrets now lies revealed. The Moors are getting their share of visitors and publicity, and most favourably surprised at what they find. Some had no idea these Moors and their villages even existed. Many who have made the discovery have decided to remain.

The Moors cannot be described as high or mountainous; indeed their highest point, on Urra Moor above Bilsdale, is only 1,490 feet (454 metres) above sea-level. Many of the higher areas are to be found in the central portion, rising in places to over fourteen hundred feet, but a large proportion lies below the thousand-foot level. It is on these bleak, windswept hills that the tough heather flourishes, at times reaching four feet high; in autumn it turns the entire surface into an enormous quilt of deep purple, broken by patches of bright green or dull brown.

There is some concern that the heather-covered moorland is disappearing – some sixty-five square miles have vanished due to horticulture and forestry work since 1950, and it is one of the tasks of the National Park Committee to strike a suitable balance between conservation of the Moors and the needs of agriculture. Another associated problem is the loss of heather due to the encroachment of bracken, a tough plant which is establishing itself on some of the lower slopes. It can bring disease to moorland sheep, but once it has taken over an area of heather, it can be eradicated only with great difficulty and at considerable expense. One solution could lie with the *Parthendes Angularis* moth, imported from South Africa, which feeds upon bracken; tests are beng conducted in selected areas.

The higher central moors, rich with their covering of heather, include those of Westerdale, Baysdale, Farndale, Glaisdale, Rosedale, Wheeldale and Danby High. They gather their waters from the rich peat depths and discharge them down their rocky slopes. Some of these streams, known as becks, run to the south to flow eventually into gentle Ryedale, while others flow north into the Esk.

Those elevated moors are rich with the remains of bygone

civilizations in the form of burial ground and entrenchments. One curious mound lies in the northerly reaches of the Park, within yards of its boundary near Moorsholm, but inside County Cleveland. It is a strange conical shape known as Freeborough Hill, whose summit is only some 820 feet above sea-level but whose profile and position at the edge of the Moors provide it with a mystique of its very own.

As a child, I understood there was a pit shaft running directly from the summit into the centre which contained hundreds of horses killed in past battles. Some say it contains many people who died during the Black Plague, and indeed a grave was found here during the last century. It was made of whinstone blocks carried three or four miles to this site. Another yarn says Freeborough Hill shelters King Arthur and twelve knights of the Round Table who lie asleep until required to save England.

There are arguments as to whether Freeborough is natural or man-made, but the name probably comes from the fact that the Anglican Courts or Freeburgh assembled here. It could be named after Freya, the goddess of fertility, or after the *frithborn*, the peace-bond or frankpledge of the Angles. There again, it is probably a product of an Ice Age, along with other conical hills like Roseberry Topping and Blakey Topping, but one legend says a giant scooped up a handful of earth and cast it here to form the hill. Some say it was the Devil, but others maintain it could have been Wade – he seems to have made other holes and hills on the Moors!

Directly south, across Eskdale, is Castleton Rigg with its impressive views. It stretches like a finger from Blakey, a name of the locality which might have been derived from Blakemoor or Blackamoor.

Near Blakey's windswept and lonely Lion Inn is the site of a former cockpit. Regular contests were held between adherents from Pickering and Kirkbymoorside to the south of the Moors, and challengers from Stokesley and Guisborough to the north and west. Hundreds of competitors and spectators would converge on this isolated moor, but its last cockfight was in 1760.

Back to the north of Eskdale, overlooking Danby village, is the site of Danby Beacon. This a lofty and rounded portion of the moors rising to more than a thousand feet with staggering views down Eskdale. It is rich with earthworks and tumuli, for prehistoric man lived on these heights.

Just below the Beacon are about a hundred disused pits, probably the remains of an ancient village, for they have clearly been positioned in an orderly manner. Land around the Beacon has revealed tools, clay urns and the cremated remains of ancient Britons as well as signs of forts and camps. Running water nearby gives added support to the theory that this was a village, and these moorland becks flow down the steep slopes to join the Esk close to the North York Moors National Park Centre at Danby, now known as 'The Moors Centre'.

Danby Beacon has been described as 'one of the lonely places of nature', but during World War II it became the site of RAF Danby Beacon, a radar station with eight tall pylons, four of metal and four of timber. They were dismantled after the war, and the station closed in the late 1950s.

One feature of the Moors between Danby and Little Fryup is a hollow on the side of Danby Rigg. This is Wolf Pit Slack, thought to have been a crossing place for wolves, and a reminder of far-off days when they ran wild on these exposed moors.

The lord of the manor recruited local householders to hunt them, and beaters were mustered from the villages. One line stretched for several miles across the moorland, sometimes as long as five miles or even more. This was flanked on rising ground by a second group, while a third party stood behind a selected wolf pit, armed with lengthy nets and other weapons. (Some pits were natural depressions in the ground or even the remains of bygone civilizations, but sometimes ditches were dug for the purpose. These could be twelve or thirteen feet deep at times, and up to a mile long.) The objective was to drive the wolves into the pit, where they would be killed.

In spite of this sustained assault upon the wolf, the species did survive, and further efforts were made to curtail their numbers. At Baysdale near Westerdale, in the fourteenth century, the land rents were paid in wolves' heads, and at one time a criminal could be freed by producing a specified number of wolves' tongues.

The Saxons were afraid of the wolf and made strenuous efforts to eradicate it. Indeed, January was known to them as '*Wulfmonath*', 'the month of the wolf'. when it was at its most hungry and dangerous, and cattle and even children were at risk. One old saying says, 'When several wolves appear together, it is not a society of peace but of war. It is attended with tumult and dreadful prowlings, and indicates an attack upon some large animal.'

But it was not the old methods of hunting that eradicated the wolf from our moors. It was the firearm. Once this gained acceptance among the hunters, the unfortunate wolf stood no chance. Within the Moors, he was rendered extinct. But the date of the last one to run wild on our moors is not certain. One was caught in Cheshire in 1509, and they are generally thought to have been made extinct further north between 1650 and 1700. Some accounts suggest the last wolf in the Lake District occurred in 1680, and as late as 1743 one was reputedly killed in Scotland, the last known wolf to live wild in Britain.

But these figures do not tell the whole story. In the early morning of a day in 1968 I found a small pack of yellow-eyed Canadian timber wolves assembled in a bus shelter near Pickering. Fortunately I was in a police car with radio, and they were docile, having escaped from a zoo. We returned them within a short time. In November 1969 one was shot near Scarborough, also an escapee!

During the autumns and winters of modern times, however, similar long lines of people can be seen beating the moors as they drive their prey towards men with guns. Those men are concealed in the many butts seen beside the moorland tracks – but they do not seek the wolf. They seek the grouse, known locally as the moor bird or moor game.

A grouse shoot is claimed to be one of the most exhilarating and one of the most skilled of sports and one which is vital to the survival of the Red Grouse. This bird not found beyond the shores of Great Britain. Unique to our islands, it lives among the heather upon which it depends for survival. It feeds on the ling, as the local heather is known, eating different parts of the plant throughout the year and its seeds in the autumn. It lives among the heather by scurrying along tracks it has created beneath the canopy of tightly knit foliage. It is a tough bird. Even in winter, it can survive beneath the snow which settles on the heather. A moderate or light fall leaves the ground beneath the thick cover of heather free and available for the grouse, although it has been known to paddle down the snow which falls on its territory, especially that which arrives in late spring. This keeps the heather exposed and available for food and shelter.

The Red Grouse is a large and rather dumpy bird, about the size of a small domestic hen, and its plumage is a rich reddish brown. It has two prominent red combs above the eyes, and its feet and legs are covered in small white feathers. It does not fly very often nor indeed very proficiently because it has short wings and a heavy body. When startled, it will literally clatter from the heather with a harsh call which sounds like 'go-back, go-back, go-back'. With a whirring of wings, it will dart and weave over the moors for a short distance, and then glide back into the secret depths of its beloved heather.

Its rapid weaving and low flight require more than ordinary skills to shoot it, and for this reason the bird is an attraction for shooting parties. Areas of the moors are let to grouse-shooting parties for extraordinarily high sums, running into thousands of pounds for a season and even hundreds for a single day. It is a costly indulgence, and it makes the grouse an expensive bird both to maintain and to shoot. In spite of these high fees, it costs a landowner money to keep the grouse upon his land. In some areas, the grouse owes its survival to the landowners who are prepared to spend money to ensure its continuing presence.

The season begins on the 'Glorious Twelfth' of August (and ends on 10 December), with shooters from the various moors vying with one another to claim the first brace. An early pair will appear on noted dinner tables on the night of the 12th, and helicopters, fast cars and aircraft are now used in the annual race to put the first grouse upon the gourmet's city table.

Grouse shooting is a vital part of the conservation process. Because grouse feed exclusively on the heather, too many birds would result in too little food, with a resultant weakening of the strain and possible extinction. Another factor is that the grouse suffers from an inherent disease which attacks and kill the weak, hungry and ailing birds. For the grouse to survive, it has to be carefully culled, and shooting is the least cruel and most effective method.

With conservation of the Red Grouse in mind, the North of England Grouse Research Project is currently conducting a computerized survey into the effects of the grouse's worm-induced disease, called strongylosis; the project was initiated with a view to making recommendations to landowners and other interested parties about future shooting requirements and breeding plans.

There is no doubt that the annual grouse shoot does fulfil a conservationist role, but in addition it provides sport and excitement. It also provides a living for many moorland people, and another subsidiary factor is that the heather must be kept in prime condition so that the grouse can feed upon it. Controlled burning is therefore undertaken between 1 November and 31 March, and this burns off the tough, old and expired heather so that a new, strong growth can establish itself. These patches of burnt heather, called swiddens or swizzens, help to provoke a fresh growth of heather to feed and shelter more generations of grouse.

But while the efforts of those interested in grouse shooting do help to conserve and protect the Moors, other recreations cause severe and even irreparable harm. Especially at risk is the vital covering of heather and peat.

This seemingly innocuous habit of picnicking can create untold damage, as was witnessed by the destructive moorland fires during the summer of 1976. A heatwave, the hottest for many years, made the moorland turf, heather and peat so dry that a burning cigarette end carelessly tossed upon it, or a picnic fire left burning or even the sun shining through the glass of a broken bottle, could cause an outbreak of fire. At risk from such an uncontrolled fire would be the heather upon which so much depends, and the thick layer of peat below it. This spongy blanket of natural goodness provides the nourishment for the moors. Also at risk is all wildlife, whether in the form of plants, insects, birds, animals or reptiles, together with the domesticated sheep which live free upon the moors. And on top of that are forests and fields, the smallholdings and even human homes and livelihoods. All are at risk and, indeed, all suffered during the moor fires of 1976.

In the two months from 27 June until 27 August that year, more than fifteen hundred fires broke out on the North York Moors. Over sixty were classified as major outbreaks, and they all affected moorland turf, stubble, grass and forestry sites. The first of these broke out on 27 June on Wheeldale Moor, near Wade's Causeway, and destroyed over four square miles of heather and forty acres of forest. Another, on the moors above Glaisdale and Rosedale, destroyed two square miles of moorland, many of the others subsequently destroying huge areas of heather and peat.

Young grouse, seeking refuge in their territories, flew back into the flames, while tiny curlews, featherless and too young to fly, could not escape the searing flames. Even man was at risk.

Moor fires can travel a long distance very quickly and, when fanned by a moorland breeze, the flames can leap across roads and whip through forests faster than a man can run. Fire warnings are a regular feature of the moors and forests, but sadly there are people who are totally oblivious to the dangers they create.

The problem is that an uncontrolled moor fire burns deep into the peat. As this can be up to thirty feet thick, a fire can therefore smoulder for months. The peat-laden earth of the moors is combustible, and long periods of heat and burning, albeit below the surface, can severely harm the moor for many future decades. Nothing will grow on the ravaged surface; wildlife cannot survive, and even human jobs and homes can be lost.

During the 1976 outbreak, silly sightseers also caused problems, because they drove onto the heights to witness the spectacular sight of miles of heather ablaze. In so doing, they put themselves and their vehicles at risk and also impeded the harrowing fire-fighting efforts. A change of wind can instantly and completely alter the situation, and during that outbreak there was even talk of evacuating some of the moorland villages deep in the dales.

At one stage, a wall of fire twenty feet high and 1½ miles wide swept towards Glaisdale Head, threatening farms and homes; a last-minute change of wind direction, aided by a sturdy dry-stone wall and a water-filled bomb crater, halted the sweeping flames. They had already blazed for twenty-four hours and had destroyed a thousand acres of moor.

In spite of gallant, unstinting work by the fire-fighters, both professional and volunteer, the only real solution was rain. Rain had to fall to penetrate the hot earth, and it had to fall in sufficient volume and for a sufficiently long time to saturate the moors. Happily, after inestimable damage, the rains did come. It was winter before the fires were finally extinguished, but it will take decades for the Moors to fully recover, if indeed, they ever do.

But out of that damage, a new but different life has emerged. As a direct result of the fires, mosses are growing on the burnt-out acres, and a rare beetle, found in only two other places in the world, has been found. Insects, mice, hares and rabbits are returning to areas newly planted where heather once dominated, and the sheep are loving the cottongrass which in some areas is the only plant to survive.

Scientists and research workers have been encouraged to examine the moors in more detail, and although that outbreak of fire did such enormous harm, nature has surprised everyone by her ability to adapt to these enforced circumstances.

Today, if you cross the moors, you will see the blackened areas of recent burning brightened by patches of fresh green moss. The sheep still graze in blissful contentment, and you will hear the curlew and the skylark. Grouse will clatter from the heather, or an adder, Britain's only poisonous snake, will bask in the sun on an exposed rock. You might even see a woodmouse, a little creature no one thought lived on these heights. Maybe it has come to live among the new trees planted in the aftermath of the fire, or perhaps it has been here for centuries, having adapted to new surroundings when ancient man cut down the trees and allowed the heather to take over.

The fires taught us a lot, and their aftermath has produced many surprises, but there is still an overriding need for visitors to think before they throw away their lighted cigarettes and matches, or light their picnic fires in such combustible surroundings. They should not forget that, while they have come to the moors for pleasure and recreation, for many people and a wide range of living things those same moors provide a home and a very precious livelihood.

Another problem has been caused by participants in the Lyke Wake Walk, albeit without malice in most cases. Their sheer numbers have begun to erode the moorland surface. The idea for this walk came to a local writer and farmer, Bill Cowley, as he climbed up to the rigg between Glaisdale and Fryup Dale. From that point there is a stunning view, a vista which reeks of romance and mystery and which is redolent of ancient times and moorland folklore. Cowley realized it was possible to walk the breadth of the moors without seeing another human being and without visiting any village or hamlet. He considered this, wrote about it and found himself issuing a challenge to anyone who would complete, on foot and within the space of twenty-four hours, the route he envisaged. He offered a trophy to anyone who could complete the walk from Scarth Nick near Swainby on the western edge of the moors to Wyke Point at Ravenscar on the east coast. The distance was forty-two miles and it meant crossing the highest and widest point of the North York Moors.

That was in 1955; the first successful crossing took place in October of that year, and by the early 1980s the Walk was attracting around twenty thousand hikers each year. They came in all seasons and from all spheres of life and points of the globe. Many came in large organized parties.

Early in its history, Cowley himself completed the walk and was reminded of the words of the Cleveland Lyke Wake Dirge, possibly Yorkshire's oldest dialect verse.

The dirge was sung at funerals, and its name comes from some old Scandinavian words. A '*wake*' means the vigil over a corpse, and '*lyke*' refers to the corpse itself. From this we get 'lych', referring to lychgates over church entrances under which the coffins would rest, and the term '*lyke wake*' refers to the watch over a corpse.

And so was born the idea of linking the walk with this dirge, for it was once believed that the souls of the dead were taken up to Whinney Moor and then to the Bridge of Death and beyond.

This ancient dirge was once known widely in various forms in the north of England, and Sir Walter Scott had his own version. In the Moors, it appears to have last been sung at a funeral in Kildale around 1800.

Referring to it in 1686, John Aubrey wrote, 'The beliefe in Yorkshire was amongst the vulgar (perhaps is in part still) that after the person's death, the soule went over Whinney Moore and till about 1616-24, at the funerale, a woman came and sang the followeing song.'

There are ten verses, but the first three are as follows:

This yah neet, this yah neet,
Ivvery neet an' all,

Firė an' fleet an' cannle leet,
An' Christ tak up thy saul.

When thoo frae hence away art passed,
Ivvery neet an' all,
Ti Whinney Moore thoo cums at last,
An' Christ tak up thy saul.

If ivver thoo gave owther hosen or shoon,
Ivvery neet an' all,
Clap thee doon, an' put 'em on,
An' Christ tak up thy saul.

To this awesome chant, some Lyke Wake walkers make that eerie crossing, now one of the set-pieces of the North York Moors.

But its popularity has caused problems. Some participants have let down Bill Cowley by chopping up fences to make fires, by knocking down walls, sleeping rough in barns and otherwise treating the moors like an urban dumping ground.

None the less, many thousands regard the Walk as a genuine, healthy challenge, but even this causes problems.

The tramp of so many well-shod feet has caused serious erosion, much of it on private land. Public footpaths along the Walk have not suffered too greatly, but in some central areas the peat layer has been worn dangerously thin, which in turn allows the remaining layers to be swept away by water or blown away in the wind. Due to the actions of the walkers, the route is no longer a mere footpath – at times it is the width of a major road, and in some parts it is up to 120 yards wide. Because peat supports the whole life cycle of the moors, its disappearance threatens their very existence. And once it has vanished, it will not return, because peat cannot be formed or grow in a modern climate.

Appeals have been made for large parties not to make the crossing, for when such numbers arrive at these wide, heatherless areas when they are wet and boggy, they tend to avoid them by walking onto the adjacent moor. This causes the route to grow wider and wider, with further destruction, and large bogs have replaced the smaller pathways in some areas.

The people are destroying the very thing they love and enjoy.

Concern for the long-term effect upon the moors has led to studies being undertaken by the North York Moors National

Park Committee and by Mr Cowley himself, but to date the walk continues. Closing it is the last thing anyone wants, and besides, it would be impossible to do so, therefore publicity has sought to reduce the number of annual crossings by twenty-five per cent. Fortunately, many groups have heeded requests to keep their organized treks to a minimum. The campaign, backed by groups like the Lyke Wake Club itself, the Country Landowner's Association, the Ramblers' Association, and the Blackfaced Sheepbreeders Association, has had a positive effect, because in the summer of 1984 it was reported that crossings had been reduced by fifty per cent. Motor cyclists are a new problem, for reckless riders both damage the moor and threaten the safety of hikers and visitors.

A similar problem has arised around the Hole of Horcum, this time due to the activities of hang-gliding enthusiasts. Their earthbound movements are causing similar erosion of the surface in that area, and it is unfortunate that the Hole of Horcum offers unrivalled facilities for lovers of this latest form of moorland sport. Fortunately, their organizers understand the problems and are also co-operating closely with the National Park authorities in an attempt to find a solution which will be agreeable to everyone who uses the moors for recreation. As I write, hang-gliding continues, albeit with stringent conditions.

But it must not be thought that the Moors are used solely for recreation. People do live there, and the Moors boast several intriguing villages.

Hutton-le-Hole, with its streams, close-cut grass and folk museum, is one of the prettiest, while Goathland is one of the best known. Lockton and Levisham recline nearby and were once known as the twin towns of the Moors. The eleventh-century Church of St Mary is almost hidden in the valley between them, one writer describing the hills as 'a breakneck descent and two distressing climbs'.

Levisham boasted a forge in 1207, and part of the moor surrounding it is known as Killingnoble Scar, once the haunt of peregrine falcons kept by James I for hawking. In 1612 the local people were charged with the duty of 'watching the birds for the King's use'. At the foot of the scar was a pool known as Newton Dale Well where long ago a Midsummer Day fair was held, and a ceremony called Blessing the Well was conducted. These waters were known for their health-giving properties, and a spa complex was proposed for the site during the last century. The notion did not reach fruition.

Levisham railway station is a couple of tortuous miles away in the lovely Newton Dale and is served by steam trains of the North York Moors Railway.

These delightful villages are worthy of anyone's attention, while far across to the west of the Moors are noteworthy places like Osmotherley, Hawnby, Old Byland and the aptly named Cold Kirby.

While most of the villages within the Moors are to be found either deep in the dales or nestling on the sheltering slopes, some, like those mentioned above, are practically on the open Moors.

Hutton-le-Hole, so popular with visitors, is midway between the Moors and the gentler plains of Ryedale, but windswept Goathland stands on an elevated plain to the south of Eskdale. Both are wide-open villages where moorland sheep roam free. Fierce arguments rage about the merits of fencing in the sheep, due to their slaughter by motor cars, not to mention large-scale thefts, and they surprise unsuspecting tourists by approaching them for titbits – I've even seen them climb into cars in their hunt for tasty morsels. But their presence is shown in another way, for the verges and open expanses of grass in and around villages like Hutton-le-Hole and Goathland are beautifully shorn. The non-stop munching of these ever-present sheep ensures smart, trimmed verges all the year round in these and many more moorland villages.

The right to graze sheep on the open moors is one which has been jealously guarded for centuries, and the moor sheep are known as 'heeafed', a dialect term meaning that each sheep recognizes its patch of moor as its 'home'.

Goathland is a fine centre for exploration. It is surrounded by splendid scenery and gorgeous waterfalls known as 'fosses', and there are magnificent woods, with precipitous cliffs and extensive moorland views. The village is the home of the Goathland Plough Stots, a long-surviving sword-dance team.

There are some remarkably fine hotels here, and the name of Goathland invariably excites interest. One popular misconception is that it is derived from goats, but the name probably comes from 'Goda's Land', Goda being the name of a Scandinavian settler. 'Gothland' is a possible source too, coming from the area's colonization by the Goths of south Sweden. Another possibility is that it comes from 'Gode Land', meaning 'God's Land', in memory of a religious foundation.

In 1117 Godeland, then within the vast Forest of Pickering, was granted by Henry I to Osmund, a priest, so that he could pray for the soul of Queen Matilda and provide lodgings for the poor. Following this, St Mary's Hermitage was established, but subsequent hard times caused it to be attached to Whitby Abbey. The modern parish church remains dedicated to St Mary, but there are no remains of that old hermitage.

One of the sights is Mallyan Spout, a fine seventy-foot-high waterfall behind the Mallyan Hotel. From there it is possible to walk to Nelly Ayre Foss, both waterfalls being on West Beck, which flows behind the village. Downstream from Goathland, on the Murk Esk, is Thomason Foss, where the river falls into a deep pool over a wall of dark rock on its way to Beckhole.

Beckhole is a lovely hamlet surrounded by nature, although between 1858 and 1864 it employed almost two hundred men in the iron-ore industry. Quoits is still played here, as it is in several moorland villages, and Beckhole boasts an original oil painting as its pub sign, the work of Sir Algernon Newton RA, father of Robert Newton, the actor famous for his portrayal of Long John Silver in the film of *Treasure Island*.

If the name of Goathland is in any way linked to Osmund and his religious establishment, it is interesting to learn that another Osmund, or perhaps the same one, had links with Osmotherley twenty-five miles away on the western edge of the Moors. This village name has always caused interest, and it may come from the Old Norse, meaning 'Osmund's Ley', a ley being a clearing. Its old name was 'Osmunderly', but there is a legend which links it with Roseberry Topping and provides another version of the name.

A local princess dreamt her son Os would die on a certain day and ordered a nurse to take him to a safe place. The summit of Roseberry Topping, then known as Odinsberg, a prominent, cone-shaped hill near Great Ayton, seemed safe enough, but in the peace of the hillside the nurse fell asleep, and the baby prince wandered away. When his nurse awoke, he was lying face down in a spring, dead. He was buried at Osmotherley. Later, at

Mount Grace Priory, his mother died from grief and was buried at his side. Thus we get the name 'Os-by-his-mother-lay'. It sounds highly improbable but makes a nice yarn.

Osmotherley is a pleasant village with modern homes and old cottages straggling side by side along the road which leads in from the A19.

Above the village is a large patch of water administered by the Yorkshire Water Authority and known officially as Cod Beck Reservoir. This miniature lake, known locally as the 'The Sheepwash', is popular with visitors, and large car-parks have been provided. Beyond is Scarth Nick, a dramatic cleft in the hills above Swainby, an impressive relic of the Ice Age.

Back in the centre of Osmotherley, however, is a marvellous old stone table, a squat structure standing next to the heavily carved market cross. It was upon this table that John Wesley stood to deliver a stirring sermon, as a result of which, in 1754, he built at Osmotherley one of the first Methodist chapels in the moors. The Anglican church has a fifteenth-century tower and porch and a long nave with medieval walls and Norman foundations, and its font is Norman. During renovations in 1892, the foundations of a Saxon apse were discovered.

On the Moors outside Osmotherley is a famous old drovers' inn called the Chequers Inn. Now a farmhouse, it stands eight hundred feet above sea-level, and the three-hundred-year-old inn proclaimed on its chequerboard sign a message which said,

Be not in haste,
Step in and taste,
Ale tomorrow for nothing.

In 1960 this sign disappeared, but it was found in Northallerton and restored to its rightful place in April 1984.

The road beyond twists, turns and dips across Snilesworth Moor, traversing streams and fords and winding through farmyards. Coaches are advised not to use this tortuous route, but it does reveal some breathtaking views on its journey to Hawnby.

John Wesley used this route on 7 July 1757 and afterwards wrote, 'I rode through one of the pleasantest parts of England to Hawnby.'

Tucked into the western edge of the Moors are many delightful villages whose farmers, over the centuries, have been able to cultivate the plains below and also run their sheep on the adjacent Moors. Those villages include Thimbleby, Over Silton, Nether Silton, Kepwick, Cowesby, Upsall and Boltby, all readily accessible. They nestle in narrow, leafy lanes, almost hidden from the world among thick vegetation and ranging woodlands. Like other, similar communities, some had religious establishments. Between Thimbleby and Over Silton (the latter described by Arthur Mee as 'a place of far horizons') there is a farm said to be built on the foundations of a medieval nunnery, while on the moors above is the Hanging Stone, a huge rock 931 feet above sea-level.

There is a curious puzzle on a stone at Nether Silton. In a field overlooked by the church and the old manor house stands a square stone pillar, well over six feet high. On the face which overlooks the Vale of Mowbray are rows of initial letters without any words, and the date AD 1765. The letters are:

HTGOMHS
TBBWOTGWWG
TWOTEWAHH
ATCLABWHEY
AD1765
AWPSAYAA

They are said to mean: 'Here the grand old manor house stood; the black beams were oak, the great walls were good; the walls of the east wing are hidden here; a thatched cottage like a barn was here erected year AD 1765; a wide porch spans a yard and alcove.'

Boltby is picturesque and peaceful. It reclines in the foothills by a rippling stream. There is a tiny humped-back bridge and a stone gatehouse of Mount St John, a house said to be upon the original site of a preceptory of the Knights Hospitallers. On the plain below is Nevison House, the legendary home of the notorious seventeenth-century highwayman William Nevison. He was christened 'Swift Nick' by Charles II, and lore says he performed the famous Black Bess ride from London to York, not Dick Turpin.

Also tucked into the beautiful foothills at the western side of the moors is the silvery water of Lake Gormire, a tarn-like lake about a third of a mile in circumference. It is remarkable because no streams run in or out of it; it is a natural lake rich with wildlife and probably dates from glacial times. A steep, winding footpath climbs down to it from Sutton Bank Top, close to the car-park and the National Park Information Centre.

As one might expect, the lake has attracted its legends. One says it is bottomless, and another claims the lake contains a village, complete with church and spire. The Devil has his place too, one story claiming that astride a white horse he leapt from the towering cliffs and crashed through the earth to form the crater which has since filled with water. Another legend says that a white mare carrying a girl leapt to its death over the cliff behind Gormire and that the body of the girl was never found. The pale cliff behind is known as White Mare Crag, and the location of a roundabout at the entrance to Thirsk on the A170 is called White Mare Corner.

On the cliff face at the far side of the Gliding Club is the carved figure of the White Horse of Kilburn, dealt with earlier (p. 81). Strangely it is not linked with the legend of the White Mare, for one theory is that 'White Mare' is a corruption of 'White Mere', referring to the shining surface of the lovely Lake Gormire.

The plains stretching inland from Sutton Bank Top are still associated with horses, but these are modern racehorses. This has long been a noted training area with fine, open gallops graced by impressive views. Racing here reached its peak of popularity in the eighteenth century: between 1715 and 1770 the annual Black Hambleton Races were staged. Racing stables continue to occupy a nearby site. The turf is said to be the best in England for training horses, and strings of exercising racehorses are a regular sight.

Soaring gliders from the nearby Yorkshire Gliding Club fill the sky when conditions are right, and the views from the ground here are staggering, perhaps the best in Yorkshire and even the best in England. They stretch into the Pennines to the west, into Cleveland to the north and into West Yorkshire to the south.

John Wesley came this way in March 1755, and William Wordsworth admired the view in July 1802. He came with his sister Dorothy and paused here during his journey to Brompton, near Scarborough, for his wedding. After his wedding, in October the same year, and now accompanied by his new wife, Mary, they paused once more, this time at dusk, before staying overnight in Thirsk.

Wordsworth wrote a sonnet about that view in which he mentioned an 'Indian citadel, Temple of Greece and Minster with its tower, substantially expressed'. Dorothy, in her journal, also mentions 'a minster unusually distinct, minerets in another quarter, and a round Grecian temple'.

Sutton Bank, a notorious hill on the A170, is a mile long with three gradients of one in five (twenty per cent), one in four (twenty-five per cent) and again one in five (twenty per cent). It presents no worries to the local motorists but seems to cause immense problems to inexperienced motorists and holiday traffic. It is inconceivable that some drivers attempt to tow caravans up this hill, but it is frequently blocked with cars and caravans during the summer season. Local drivers avoid it for this reason, and from the summer of 1984 caravans were banned from Sutton Bank.

The walks and vistas from the top are breathtaking. There is a walk around the edge of the cliffs towards the Yorkshire Gliding Club from where one can see Hood Hill in the valley below – Hood was where the monks of Byland first settled in Yorkshire, and the same hill was long ago thought to be the site of human sacrifices.

At the top of Sutton Bank, close to the path of the old drovers' road, a massive bonfire was lit on 6 June 1977 to commemorate the Silver Jubilee of Her Majesty Queen Elizabeth II. It was Number 82 in a chain of 103 fires stretching from Jersey in the Channel Isles to Saxavord in the Shetlands. The first to be lit was at Windsor Castle, and I was present when Sutton Bank's flames flooded the lofty site twenty minutes later.

The old drovers' road which passed nearby entered the Moors near Swainby on the north-west before running almost due south. It passed along the heights of Black Hambleton where it ran close to Sutton Bank Top. There the road forked, one track descending into the upper Ryedale near Oldstead and going on towards York via Coxwold, and the other following what is now the A170 (Thirsk to Scarborough road) to Tom Smith's Cross above Ampleforth. It then bore right off the A170 and ran along the road still known as Ampleforth High Street, which in fact is about a mile out of the village. It ran down to Ampleforth Beacon and through Oswaldkirk Bank Top, Stonegrave and Hovingham into lower Ryedale and Malton. Today, some stretches have been surfaced and are used as modern highways, while others on the Moors remain a green road or rough track which is fascinating to walk upon. It provides a wonderful sense of history, together with spectacular views.

The name is slightly misleading, because this lofty route was a track long before droving began. It was part of an ancient route between Scotland and London and existed long before the Great North Road which now slices through North Yorkshire. Its precise age is unknown; some authorities believe it is prehistoric. Evidence of Bronze Age man has been found close to the route, and an Iron Age fort was discovered near Boltby; earthworks and dykes have been found alongside or even crossing the southern tip of the road. It is also fairly certain that the Romans used it. They did not pave it in the style of their famous road upon Wheeldale Moor, but Roman remains have been found both at the northern and southern end of the Hambleton Drove Road.

It is highly probable that the Saxons and Norsemen used it and that William the Conqueror followed this route in 1069 after completing his Harrying of the North. He marched from Teesside to York in a terrible snowstorm, during which he got lost in the Bilsdale area. Similarly, when St Cuthbert's body was being carried around the north of England, it was probably borne along here to Crayke, where it rested awhile. Another user must have been Edward II, who fled after his army was defeated at Scots Corner in 1322. This battle site is above Oldstead and is just off the route of this ancient track.

During the Middle Ages, it would have been used by foot passengers and horsemen who visited or traded with local monasteries and abbeys, and it survived throughout the sixteenth century, when landowners were duty bound to maintain the roads which ran within their parishes.

In 1663 the road from York to Coxwold became a turnpike road as far as Oldstead, but beyond that point the ancient route across the Hambleton Hills did not change, remaining an unmade track. But as the coaches made use of the new turnpike roads, traffic upon the Hambleton road began to decline. For the men who drove cattle from Scotland, an ancient track like the Hambleton Road provided a marvellous cross-country route. It was direct, and there were no tolls but plenty of inns along its length. Furthermore, it was wide with expansive grass verges to facilitate the movement and welfare of both cattle and drovers. So this old route found a new role as a Drove Road.

Although cattle droving had been practised since medieval times, it reached its peak upon the Moors in the eighteenth and nineteenth centuries. To feed the ever-growing population of London, hundreds of thousands of cattle were required, and this prompted a massive movement of animals, all on foot. Those which used this route from Scotland were intended for the markets of Malton and York, although some went into the Midlands and eventually London. There were well-used halts along the route for both man and beast, and along the fifteen-mile stretch in the North York Moors there were four drovers' inns. One still functions as an inn. This is the Hambleton Inn near the top of Sutton Bank on the side of the A170, close to the National Park Information Centre. Another was Limekiln House located above Kepwick on Black Hambleton; this served both drovers and lime workers who quarried nearby. It is now a ruin. Close to the northern end was the famous Chequers Inn mentioned on page 97. This is now a farm, as is the fourth inn, Dialstone Farm, not far from Sutton Bank Top on the road to Cold Kirby, which provides a fine view of this ancient track.

The drovers seemed to have been welcomed by the local people, for they brought news and money into the remote moorland villages. Furthermore, because the animals required treatment and shoeing, many wayside craftsmen earned a good living from these passing armies of men and beasts. Sometimes a procession of cattle would be up to two miles long, comprising thousands of animals.

It is interesting to note that on one occasion, at Sutton Bank Top, a drover was passing with his cattle just as William Wordsworth and his sister Dorothy were walking there. The date was 1802, and Dorothy wrote about 'the little Scotch cattle' which panted and tossed fretfully about. These cattle were driven with the help of dogs, and there are stories of dogs being sent home alone upon completion of a drive. On the way to Scotland, the solitary dog would visit the various inns to be fed, and the cost would be met by its owner during the next journey.

It was not only cattle which were driven here, however. Pigs, sheep, turkeys and geese used this route, invariably to avoid the cost of the turnpikes. Indeed, it was used this century for the driving of animals from Ryedale to the sheep sales at Swainby. And in 1984 the road is still in use; some lengths have been surfaced for use by modern traffic, while the unsurfaced portions have been adopted as the Cleveland Way, a long-distance footpath.

The end of long-distance droving came with the advent of the railway and modern shipping. The changed methods of transporting cattle, with progress in the canning industry and meat refrigeration, made these long-distance treks unnecessary.

But this and other ancient tracks enable us to see the Moors as they were many centuries ago. I suspect they have changed very little.

6

'Twixt heather and sea

'The field is full of shades as I near the shadowy coast.'
Francis Thompson (1859–1907)

The modern Englishman enjoys his coast. It offers sunshine and space, with the scent of the waves and a promise of distant lands.

The North Yorkshire coastline supplies these requirements and furthermore is dramatic and picturesque, with beaches that are undoubtedly superior to many because they comprise miles of pleasant, clean sand. But this coast suffers one set-back – it is often shrouded in a chilling, dense and damp fog or mist, known locally as a 'sea-fret' or a 'roak'. But catch any point of this coast on a fine, warm, sunny day and you've got the best in England.

This inspiring and scenic coastline is enriched along its length with rocky portions called nesses, nabs, wykes and scaurs. It follows an irregular path as it takes in the classic resorts of Scarborough and Whitby, with famous fishing villages such as Staithes, Runswick Bay and Robin Hood's Bay nestling along its length. In addition, there are some of England's finest beaches and loftiest cliffs.

It begins at Staithes in the north and ends a few miles south of Filey; indeed, this stretch of about thirty-five miles now technically encompasses the entire Yorkshire coastline. The counties of West Yorkshire and South Yorkshire do not have any coast, and one effect of the county boundary changes of 1974 was to place the portion south of Reighton, near Filey, in the new county of Humberside. North of Staithes, a ten-mile stretch passed into County Cleveland.

Another effect of the boundary changes was to remove some of England's highest cliffs from Yorkshire and place them in County Cleveland, and to donate the majesty of Flamborough to Humberside.

But Yorkshire traditionalists, mindful of that great era before 1974, will continue to say that the full Yorkshire coastline begins near Middlesbrough in the north and terminates at Spurn Head in the south. Few would argue with them.

So far as the map is concerned, however, the Yorkshire coast (which means the North Yorkshire coast) does begin at Staithes in the north and does finish between Reighton and Bempton in the south.

In spite of the boundary changes, North Yorkshire has retained a great deal, and some twenty-six miles of captivating coastline are on the seaward side of the Moors.This provides a beautiful eastern border graced by long, smooth beaches and dramatic cliffs but it must not be forgotten that the North Sea, with its powerful currents and rapidly rising tides, can be unexpectedly threatening and even dangerous. This powerful sea has conquered ships and sent men to their deaths, just as furious waves have caused the tall cliffs to crumble, taking houses and people with them. It is not surprising that the tiny coastal communities are among the most romantic and fascinating in the realm; their people live daily with adventure, romance and danger.

These villages are literally 'twixt heather and sea', as local publicity says, but there are some differences and no little confusion between the National Park boundaries and the county boundaries which apparently ignore each other. For example, the lofty Boulby Cliffs, near Staithes, England's highest at 690 feet (209 metres), are in County Cleveland but are situated in the North York Moors National Park. Indeed, this new county includes some of the National Park's finest moorland acreage and two lovely reservoirs, Lockwood Beck and Scaling Dam. Another anomaly is that Staithes' lifeboat house stands in

County Cleveland but the village is in North Yorkshire, separated only by a narrow stream. Further south, the National Park excludes the port of Whitby and some of its neighbouring villages, as it also excludes Scarborough and its satellite communities.

But for the purpose of this book, the coast from Staithes almost to Scarborough will be included, for this is the portion which abuts the Moors.

So how can 'the coast' be defined? Fortuitously, man has provided a very suitable marker, one which conveniently divides the coast from the Moors. It is the road from Guisborough to Scarborough. From the north, it enters North Yorkshire near Staithes, where it is classified as the A174. It then hugs the coastline, passing perilously close to the sea as it edges through Sandsend before entering Whitby. From Whitby, it emerges as the A171, having there joined the moor road from Guisborough, and it follows a southerly route away from the cliffs into Scarborough. The rugged stretch of cliffs between Whitby and Scarborough was considered unsuitable for a road, although engineers managed to build a remarkable railway along and through summits, and around its coves. Here the road sweeps inland some distance from the sea, but all on its seaward side from Staithes to Scarborough can be regarded as 'coast' for the purposes of this book.

I will begin with Staithes.

Old Staithes lies below the rim of the cliffs, neatly concealed from prying eyes, and it retains the aura of an olde worlde fishing community. It is not surprising that artists come to live and work here, for it emits all the sensations of a bygone fishing and sea-faring age. The older parts cluster around its tiny harbour and only by walking from the modern streets down the steep gradient can Staithes be truly appreciated. Wisely, tourists' cars and coaches are forbidden to make this trip.

Once described as narrow and painfully ill-paved, the steep hill effectively separates the old Staithes from the new as it descends from the car-park and enters a conglomeration of tiny cottages, steep steps and narrow alleyways. The houses are packed so tightly that there is little or no room for extensions or even gardens. All the buildings appear to huddle against one another for protection against the threatening sea, and even so, tiers of them descend so close to the waves that they appear liable to be swept away. Indeed, on one occasion thirteen houses were washed into the sea, and in 1953 the Cod and Lobster Inn at the edge of the sea was severely damaged by freak tides.

Regular battles with the sea are a constant feature of Staithes life, and the harbourside air is replete with the scent of sea and fish and the cries of ever-circling gulls.

The whiff of fish and seaweed reminds us that Staithes remains a closely knit community of working fisherfolk. They have been thrust into the twentieth century by the arrival of sightseers and tourists, but such intrusion has not yet spoilt this remarkable village. It retains its fascinating characteristics and has avoided the horrors of amusement arcades, dodgems and seaside bingo halls. None the less, tourism has become an essential part of the village economy, and it has been suggested that, as the number of visitors increases, the number of full-time fishermen decreases. There is little doubt that tourists provide an easier and more profitable source of income than the fierce North Sea which dominates Staithes.

But it hasn't always been popular with visitors. One guidebook of the 1880s described it as 'highly picturesque and highly unsavoury' because it was then a noted herring station with smokehouses for drying them built into the cliffs. Furthermore, fish were also cured on the beach. After being soaked in brine and pickle, they were laid out to dry, and it was this redolent atmosphere which so vividly impressed that writer. (It must have been somewhat memorable because more authors of the time referred to it.)

The curing was done by women, who also prepared the fishing lines, repaired the nets and ensured there was sufficient bait. The men manned the village fleet of cobles, the small, open fishing boats. Their catches went to major British towns, and the men used to build their own boats. These ranged from the small cobles to colliers and even whaling ships. With all this activity, there is little wonder the residents were described as 'busy as sand martins'.

It was to this busy, sea-bound village that young James Cook came around 1740, as apprentice to a grocer called Sanderson. His shop was washed away long ago but a house in the village bears a sign commemorating the great Captain Cook who discovered Australia and made many noted voyages. I was present to witness the residents' pride when that plaque was unveiled by His Royal Highness Prince Charles, the Prince of Wales, on 31 May 1978, as part of the 250th anniversary celebrations of the birth of Captain Cook.

But local rumour suggests that Cook's career did not have a very auspicious start. It has been hinted that he had to leave Mr Sanderson's shop because he stole a shilling. This is countered by the fact that he did behave correctly by obtaining a discharge before walking into Whitby to study maritime navigation. One account says he noticed a South Sea Company's shilling in the till and exchanged it for one of his own, and that the sight of that coin triggered his desire to travel. But whatever the truth about the shilling, James Cook did grow up to become a great navigator, explorer and seaman, and his achievements mean that Staithes will never be allowed to forget he started his professional life behind the counter of the village grocer's shop.

However, the uniqueness of Staithes is not confined to its extraordinary location or its links with Captain Cook. It has some customs of its very own and, indeed, a local dialect confined to the village. For example, pronunciation of 'Staithes' by the local people confuses outsiders when they call it 'Steears', with its inhabitants being known as 'Steears-ers'.

One of its customs is the wearing of a white sash with a black line at the funerals of older residents, and another practice is that some of the women still wear the traditional Staithes bonnet. This can sometimes be seen at funerals but it is also worn as a normal item of headgear. The latter custom does tend to be confined to the older ladies; none the less, it is pleasing to note that younger ones are helping to sustain the practice. The bonnet's purpose is uncertain. It may have been a means of protection against the hazards of fishing lines, for it was once worn by fisherwomen the length of the Yorkshire coast. For perhaps a century or more, however, it has been restricted to Staithes, where it is still made, even appearing in tourist shops.

For all this tradition, Staithes does not have a very ancient history. There is no parish church, although records date to 1415 and confirm it was then known as 'Staithe', the word meaning a 'landing place'. It was in fact the landing place for nearby Seaton, which has disappeared to give birth to Hinderwell.

One legend which has been allowed to fade away tells of the time Staithes was visited by two mermaids. They were caught in the harbour and locked up for several months by the worried villagers, who were not sure what they were and why they were visiting the village. Eventually the mermaids escaped and returned to the sea, but before swimming to freedom, they put a curse on Staithes by saying, 'The sea shall flow to Jackdaw's Well.' Jackdown's Well was inland, which implied that Staithes would one day be washed completely into the sea. A good deal of it has gone already, but in spite of those mythical mermaids there is still much to see and enjoy.

Walks around the village, including the Cleveland Way, take visitors into the countryside or along the cliffs, and one follows the beach to Port Mulgrave. This is dangerous to the inexperienced walker, for it allows only twenty minutes to get around the cliff foot. Try it if you dare, but beware of fast-rising tides and tumbling sections of the cliff.

Port Mulgrave is a collection of plain houses on the clifftop. The cliffs are of muddy brown earth with a rough, steep path down to the harbour, while the village is by no means beautiful. However, the miniature harbour is interesting. It was built in the middle of the last century to cope with the iron-ore boom and is now disused except by a handful of local boats. Repeated efforts are made to restore it, but it will be a difficult task – access from the land is a major problem.

Overlooking its quiet waters is the sealed-off mouth of a tunnel which once ran a mile or so into the cliff, a reminder that this decaying little complex was constructed during the peak days of iron-ore mining. It then handled some three thousand tons of ore every week, and it was through this tunnel that ore reached the harbourside for transmission to the ironworks of Jarrow-on-Tyne.

Half a mile inland from Port Mulgrave, Hinderwell straddles the A174 and was once a major community in this corner of North Yorkshire. It is now a quiet village with the aura of a small market town, and its distant past has links with Whitby through St Hilda.

The village was once known as Hilderwell, the location of St Hilda's Well, and it is over fairly recent years that the village name has been corrupted into Hinderwell. In 1808, for example, it was still called Hilderwell but was 'corruptly known at the time as Hinderwell'. Over the years, it has variously been known as Hylderwell, Hildrewell, Hynderwell and Hilderwell before acquiring its current name. Scandinavian influences in the name suggests the village is of considerable age. In the Domesday Book, it was described as wasteland, being originally known as Seaton; the manor of Seaton was closer to Staithes, and there is still a Seaton Hall near Staithes.

One of Hinderwell's modern links with St Hilda is through the parish church, built in 1773, which is dedicated to her. St Hilda is said to have blessed the ancient well in the churchyard when she was abbess of Whitby. At Hinderwell she maintained a cell so she could pray in solitude, and there used to be a 'toft' in Hinderwell whose occupants had to maintain a lamp burned before the High Altar of Whitby Abbey.

Clinging to nearby cliffs is Runswick Bay, another of North Yorkshire's delightful fishing villages. As at so many along this coast, access to the older and original parts is by descending a steep hill.

This winsome village is replete with weekend or holiday cottages, shops and the inevitable car-park on the clifftop, all due to tourism. There is a fine, sandy beach which stretches around the sheltered bay towards Kettleness, and this bay hosts many pleasure craft and a few fishing boats.

In common with other coastal villages, Runswick has suffered in dramatic sea storms. One of them washed away a complete ironworks, comprising two furnaces, an engine house and a chimney. And it seems that, if the cottages avoided the clutches of the sea, the cliffs got them. As the sea undermined the cliffs, they tended to slide into the waves, taking houses and people with them. In a landslide of 1682, the whole village, with the exception of one house, perished in a storm after sliding down the cliff – surprisingly, no lives were lost. Although new defences keep the sea at bay, the landslips continue and most of this coastline has suffered from them over the years.

Like many of the isolated inland communities and insular seaside villages, Runswick was riddled with folklore and superstition. There are tales of boats being burned after a sea tragedy and of cats being sacrificed as the fishing cobles returned from their trips, the purpose being to ensure a safe landing. As the boats came in, children would dance around clifftop fires and sing their songs to ward off impending bad weather. The children would sing:

Souther, wind, souther,
Blow father home to mother.

One oft-repeated tale concerns the Runswick Hob, one of many who haunted the North York Moors. Hobs were legendary elf-like creatures who occupied moorland farms and helped by performing hard, manual work. But the Runswick Hob lived in a cave on the shores of the bay, and his haunt was known as Hob Hole. (Hob Holes is still shown on the map. although the original cave was destroyed many years ago by jet diggers.) The women of Runswick believed in his existence and adopted him as a cure for whooping cough in their children, known locally as 'kink-cough'. At low water, a mother would carry her ailing child to the mouth of the cave and invoke the help of the Hob by chanting:

Hob hole Hob,
My bairn's gotten t'kink-cough,
Tak it off, tak it off.

Another reputed cure was to take the child onto the Moors behind the village and cut a hole in the turf. The sufferer's mouth was held close to the newly revealed earth in the belief that the smell of it would cure the cough. The Hob belief died out before 1900, but the turf-smelling idea persisted well into the early years of this century.

Dominating Runswick Bay on the eastern side is the jutting bulk of Kettleness Point, almost four hundred feet high. Long ago it supported a Roman signalling station, and now there is a coastguard station, a ruined chapel and a few straggly cottages, but little else apart from unrestricted views across the sea and along the coast.

These cliffs used to contain iron ore in their bases, and the resultant excavations caused the cliffs to collapse. On 17 December 1829 a mass of Kettleness cliff sank into the sea, taking the entire hamlet with it. It seems to have been a gentle slide into the ocean because the inhabitants had time to gain the safety of an alum ship which was standing off shore. But their homes and the alum works were overwhelmed. The alum works were rebuilt in 1831, but the alum-rich cliff face caught fire and burned for two whole years.

In 1857 more excitement came to Kettleness when the fossil remains of an ichthyosaurus and plesiosaurus were found here in a bed of alum. To match this, in 1824 the fossil remains of a teleosaurus were found at Saltwick, the other side of Whitby.

The odd name 'kettle' may come from the name of an Icelandic adventurer, but the area was known locally as the haunt of fairies known as 'bogles'. They were said to wash their linen in Claymore Well at Kettleness, and it was said, 'The noise of their bittles was heard two miles away.' A bittle was a flat board with a handle, rather like a squat cricket bat, and it was used by those without a mangle to beat clothes and linen.

It was in 1918 that the Roman fort was discovered, to fuel speculation that it marked the end of the Roman road across Wheeldale Moor. It comprised a square ditch nearly four feet deep by twelve feet wide, and this was crossed by a causeway giving access to the fort. Later, excavations revealed skulls, cloth, ox bones, the remains of domestic animals, food and coins of the reigns of the Emperors Eugenius (AD 392–4) and Honorius (AD 395–423).

Next along the coast is the village of Lythe, noted for its long, steep hill called Lythe Bank which drops dramatically into Sandsend, with impressive views along the coast to Whitby, and for Mulgrave Castle which is concealed by trees and hills. In Mulgrave's beautiful woods were glens like Wizard's Glen, Devil's Bridge, the Waterfall and Eagles' Nest.

Squatting on the top of Lythe Bank is the parish church dedicated to St Oswald. A rugged structure founded in Saxon times, it has endured several restorations, and its walls are now stout enough to withstand the rigours of the fierce coastal gales. Today it overlooks the North Sea with the solemn perseverance of a bulldog, the same sea which, during the First World War, delivered the bodies of seven sailors to the shore below. Those seamen have never been identified and are buried within the churchyard.

One of Lythe's noted priests was John Fisher, a friend of St Thomas More and the man who defied Henry VIII during the Reformation. Born in Yorkshire at Beverley, he was a distinguished scholar and famous bishop, becoming Chancellor at Cambridge in 1504, and Bishop of Rochester. His stand against Henry's Church reforms cost him his life. In 1534, when he was in prison, Pope Paul III created him a cardinal, but he was executed at Tower Hill, London, on 22 June 1535. He was canonized in 1935.

Today Lythe church is Anglican and the family place of worship of the Earls of Mulgrave, whose magnificent castle stands sheltered by trees on its prime site which overlooks the sea.

In Lythe village there is a tiny smithy whose anvil can be seen through the windows. Here is practised an old custom known as Firing the Stiddy, which celebrates all the notable anniversaries and events in the family of the Marquis of Normanby who occupy Mulgrave Castle. The stiddy, or anvil, is carried outside the forge, and wooden plugs are primed with gunpowder, then fired on the stiddy with a twenty-foot-long iron rod heated in the fire of the smithy. This event does not occur very often; I recall the stiddy being fired in 1951 to mark the wedding of the present Marquis and Marchioness of Normanby, in 1954 for the birth of their eldest son, in 1971 when it marked a visit by helicopter of the Duchess of Gloucester, and in 1975 on the occasion of the coming of age of the Earl of Mulgrave.

Outside the smithy, the A174 slices through Lythe before dropping steeply into Sandsend, location of a Roman cement works and a concentration of houses prettily arranged by the sea. It is very aptly named, for it is situated at the end of Whitby Strand and literally markes the end of Whitby's 2½ miles of graceful sandy beach.

Sandsend is hardly a suburb of Whitby, for there are two miles of open road, a golf course and some fields between them. In spite of its attractions, it does not lie within the boundaries of the National Park, but it should not be overlooked. Its quiet charms are most refreshing, and when our children were tiny, we spent happy holidays on its peaceful, safe beach.

In fact, Sandsend is really two small communities: Sandsend itself is one, and the other is a cluster of cottages called East Row, known in Viking times as Thordisa. Each has a stream which flows from the Moors near Ugthorpe. East Row Beck joins the sea near East Row, while that which emerges at Sandsend and flows over the beach is called Mickleby Beck. These parallel becks flow through heavily wooded slopes around Mulgrave Castle, passing the sites of both the old ruined castle and the modern building with its splendid gardens.

Sandsend has said farewell to its old railway viaduct with its towering iron pillars; this disappeared soon after the closure of the impressive coastal line which carried trains above the beach and houses, but reminders are there in the huge concrete bases of the massive metal uprights, and there are further remains of this incredible railway such as tunnels and cuttings. Part of its track is used by hikers, where it forms part of the Cleveland Way to provide breathtaking views of the sea and coastline.

Once through Sandsend, the A174 runs virtually along the edge of the sea and carries the road into Whitby, a town which offers unrivalled opportunities for visiting moors, rivers, glens and coast.

There is a lovely story about this stretch of road – it may be a mixture of fact and fiction but, to substantiate it, on the approaches to Whitby at Newholm Lane end stands a sturdy stone cottage, once a tollbooth, a relic of the first road between Whitby and Sandsend.

The story involves the Maharajah Duleep Singh who was exiled from India in 1849. He leased Mulgrave Castle for four years while the Marquis of Normanby was in London and went hawking on the Moors in oriental dress. He was accompanied by two Indians who cared for the hawks, and six English gamekeepers in red uniforms. At the time, there was no road along the coast between Sandsend and Whitby, and so he arranged for one to be constructed. It is said he did so because his elephants did not like walking on the beach. The tale of the elephants is not substantiated but the road is a reminder of this unusual character's brief sojourn in the area. There could be some truth in the elephant link because the beaches of the area were used as roads at low tide. A Whitby man who died in 1920 recalled a coach and four being driven along the beach from Sandsend to Whitby to attend a wedding.

Whitby's place in the religious, maritime and literary history of England is already assured. Although it lies just outside the National Park boundaries, it is surrounded on three sides by the moors and on the fourth by the North Sea. Its location is such that in the height of summer, the sun can be observed rising over the sea in the east, and later setting over the sea in the west. To stand on the British mainland and witness both events occurring over the sea is sufficiently unusual to attract early morning spectators to Whitby's piers and to draw them back again in the evening.

The town is truly 'twixt moor and sea', and some would say that this has restricted its communication with the rest of England. Whether this is good or bad is arguable, but its prime position at the mouth of the River Esk has made it into a port of stature. Even today, its role as a busy north-east port continues, and it is 'twinned' with Port Stanley on the Falkland Islands; Whitby, Ontario; Anchorage in Alaska, and Nuku A'lota, Tonga.

Whitby's part in the religious history of this country has already been recounted in Chapter 3, and its literary associations, through the poet Caedmon, form part of that history.

In the years since Caedmon, the town has continued to attract authors of many generations and styles. Although Whitby's literary associations are too many to chronicle in full, the following are worthy of mention. Mrs Elizabeth Gaskell features the town as Monkshaven in her *Sylvia's Lovers*, a book said to have inspired Tennyson. Furthermore, the illustrations in that volume are the work of George du Maurier, who used Whitby as the setting for his sketches, not realizing that the fictitious Monkshaven was indeed Whitby.

The du Mauriers loved the town. George, the author of *Trilby* in addition to being an artist and *Punch* illustrator, spent long holidays here with his family; one son, Guy, became a soldier and playwright, while the other, Gerald, became an actor who was later knighted. Daphne du Maurier, famous for her novel *Rebecca* and other stories of Cornwall, is his granddaughter.

Mary Linskill, a Whitby girl of humble origins, made her name as a novelist with *The Haven under the Hill* and *Between the Heather and the Northern Sea*. When she was four years old, Charles Dickens visited Whitby over Easter 1844. He was staying at Mulgrave Castle as a guest of Lord Normanby and visited Whitby Abbey. He also explored the quaint narrow streets, where he lunched at the 'White Horse and Griffin' in Church Street. Later, he dedicated his novel *Dombey and Son* 'with great esteem to the Marchioness of Normanby'.

Ethel Kidson's book *Herring Fleet* features the same inn and Wilkie Collins referred to it as 'the one inn of Whitby', but it has since gone. Perhaps it was Dickens who persuaded Wilkie Collins to take a holiday in Whitby – in 1861 he wrote to Dickens about the charms of the town. (Collins was the author of *The Woman in White* and *The Moonstone*.)

Bram Stoker used Whitby's cliff top graveyard as a setting in his famous *Dracula*, and this, along with the 199 steps up to the abbey, were filmed in a sequence about the infamous count in which he survived a shipwreck and raced up those steps in the form of a dog.

Naomi Jacob went to school here, as did Storm Jameson, who disguises her home town as 'Danesacre'. Dora M. Walker wrote *They Labour Mightily* about the fishermen, and Leo Walmsley of Robin Hood's Bay (which he called Bramblewick) made his name with *Three Rivers*, later filmed as *The Turn of the Tide*.

Even the famous Captain James Cook can be classed as a Whitby author, for he sailed from here and penned his *Voyages*, an account of his adventures around the world.

There are many other books and many other authors who have made use of the town, including Winifred Holtby, the author of *South Riding*.

The town has inspired songs too. Eileen Newton wrote 'Somewhere a voice is calling', and her cottage can be seen at Newholm. She also wrote educational books for a German readership in which Whitby was referred to as 'Silver Bay'. Bing Crosby's song 'The Bells of St Mary's' was said to have been inspired by the bells of Whitby's curious parish church, whose interior is more like a ship than a church, probably because it was done by ships' carpenters. One old book says, 'The ugliness of the exterior should not daunt visitors from an inspection of the interior, which is even uglier.'

Beyond the town, Canon J.C.Atkinson featured the Danby district in his classic *Forty Years on a Moorland Parish*; Major F. Fairfax-Blakeborough of Westerdale, an authority on horseracing and country life, wrote extensively about the same area of Eskdale, and James Herriot has brought the moors character to life in his worldwide-selling books about the work of a veterinary surgeon. Many of his tales are based on the western area of the Moors, around Kilburn, Coxwold and Ampleforth.

Coxwold is, of course, noted for its links with Laurence Sterne, while Stonegrave is the home of the modern novelist Piers Paul Read and his poet father, the late Sir Herbert Read.

And there are others too numerous to list.

If the ancient abbey of Streonshalh and its divinely inspired poet helped to spawn this literary outburst, then Whitby's fame is consolidated by its links with the sea. At that time of Caedmon's writing, it was still known as 'Streonshalh', which Bede interpreted as 'Bay of the Pharos', a *pharos* being a lighthouse. Another theory is that 'Streone' was the name of a person, and 'hal' or 'hall' referred to a hollow, the name therefore meaning 'Streone's Hollow'. Streona was a nickname of Eadric, a king of Mercia slain in 1017. Interestingly, there is a suburb of York called Strensall, which is a different spelling of the same name, and one wonders if this same Streone or Streona possessed another hollow or nook of land there.

It was under that name that the abbey prospered and expanded, so much so that by AD 713 it was noted the world over as a centre of learning.

Meanwhile, the citizens of this little town set about earning their living from the sea, and in this they were eminently successful. They became noted boat-builders and fishermen, two skills which remain a vital part of the town's economy to this day. The fishing boats continue to sail from its quays, the port is thriving, and a new marina has been opened in the upper harbour. In a town which suffers badly from unemployment, such developments are important, for although tourism is a major source of income, it cannot support the whole town. Diversification of skills is necessary. The workforce must be enterprising, but Whitby's people *are* enterprising. The town has experienced many peaks and troughs throughout its history, and if they are now suffering one of their many troughs, a peak will surely come. It always has. Even as this book is being compiled, plans are going ahead to build a replica of Captain Cook's *Endeavour*, and it is hoped to extend the North York Moors Railway into Whitby to boost tourism.

Even when the abbey dominated the town, the people earned their living in the way they wanted, and not as the abbey authorities dictated. Certainly the abbey did provide employment, but the town appears to have been a wealthy place in its own right.

Even so, it remained a small community. In 1536 Leland described Whitby as 'a great fischer towne', but by 1540 it boasted only some two hundred inhabitants. The first real boom in industry and population followed Sir Thomas Challoner's discovery of alum in the Cleveland Hills. As more alum was found along the coast, men and their families moved in to find work. By 1390 there were some three thousand living in Whitby. The eighteenth century brought whaling to the town and a renewal of shipbuilding, and in the nineteenth century Queen Victoria's love of jet jewellery provided another boost of employment. Started in 1800, the jet industry employed fifteen hundred men by 1856, a tenth of the population. In 1873 there were two hundred jet jewellery shops in Whitby, but the fad faded when cheap Spanish jet, far inferior, began to flood the market. By 1921 the trade had virtually disappeared although isolated craftsmen do remain.

Shipping continued, however, and by the nineteenth century, Whitby was the seventh busiest port in the kingdom, with the railways beginning to offer the town as a popular tourist resort.

As a shipbuilding town between the mid-eighteenth and mid-nineteenth centuries, Whitby was the most prosperous along this stretch of coast. To the north Staithes and Saltburn were known for their smugglers, while in the south Filey and Bridlington were small fishing communities. Even Scarborough had fewer inhabitants than Whitby. Whitby's boom in shipbuilding was so successful that young men abandoned their traditional fishing work to build ships, and their handiwork was noted for strength and durability. Their early wooden ships were tough enough to withstand the ice of the Arctic regions, and so they were used by Scoresby's whaling expeditions. Captain Cook's ships were built here too. His *Endeavour* weighed only 370 tons and carried a crew of 84, his *Resolution* was 462 tons with a crew of 112, and the *Adventure* was 336 tons with a crew of 81.

Most of the Whitby-built ships were smaller than 400 tons due to the difficulty of getting them out of the harbour. The early narrow bridge frustrated the passage of larger vessels, a feature which still applies to Whitby's present curious and ailing swing bridge.

But Whitby's shipbuilding added to its population. Soon it was around ten thousand, with a thousand earning a living from the sea.

In Whitby's strong ships, many seafarers from the town have made their impact upon the outside world. The achievements of Captain Cook are well chronicled, but others worthy of mention include William Scoresby, Luke Fox and Captain Stephen Wharton.

Scoresby was a pioneer of whaling and sailed out of Whitby annually for thirty years on his expeditions to the Arctic. He captured more whales than any other person of his day, and he devised the ships' look-out which has since become known as the 'crow's nest'.

Luke Fox, who is buried near the abbey, was the man who hunted in vain to find the North-West Passage and revived the attempts to locate it. He failed, even after sailing from London in a tiny ship to seek it. Other explorers of the calibre of Frobisher, Davis and Frankin failed, and it was Amundsen who in 1903–6 first navigated this route which links the Atlantic and Pacific Oceans round North America.

Captain Stephen Wharton set up a notable 'first' because he was the first person to carry elephants on board ship! He died in 1904, aged eighty-nine, and claimed he carried to Van Diemen's Land the two leaders of the Irish Rebellion of 1848, Cuffy and Duffey. But the elephant record happened because he was off the coast of India when the Mutiny broke out. The rebels were in possession of all the elephants, and Captain Wharton was asked if he would carry some of them from Moulmein. With the help of General Benson, another Whitby man, he managed to get some elephants on board and was rewarded with a handsome gold watch and chain, suitably inscribed.

If elephants seemed large to carry on board, it was other leviathans which created wealth for the town. Whale fishing began in Whitby in 1753, and there was an added incentive because the Government provided a bounty on whale oil. Scoresby, for example, brought home oil worth over £100,000. But by 1837, it was all over. The boom had finished. The Government withdrew its county scheme as mineral oils came into wider use, and so the profits from whaling decreased, causing the whale fisheries to close.

It was at this time that the Whitehall shipyards of Whitby began to build iron ships. The first was the SS *Whitehall*, launched on 20 June 1871; later, steel replaced iron, and Whitby's first steel ship, *Dora*, was launched in 1887.

But Whitby's harbour could not cope with larger vessels, and when the authorities refused to build a wider bridge to permit access to larger ships, orders fell off. In 1902 the Whitehall shipyards were sold. One by one they closed, and over three thousand workers left the town to find work elsewhere. A wider, swing bridge was built in 1908, but it was too late. Whitby wasn't building any big new ships to sail through it.

Today that fascinating bridge swings open to the gaze of interested visitors and permits access to the upper harbour by some moderately sized timber-carrying vessels. But at the higher end of the harbour is yet another new bridge. Opened on 21 March 1980, by the Marquis of Normanby, Lord Lieutenant of North Yorkshire, it carries through-traffic away from Whitby's narrow streets and its troublesome old bridge to provide panoramic views of this ancient town. Let's hope it watches over Whitby's next rise to prosperity.

As things are, the view embraces a curious mixture of buildings. There are the old, narrow streets which have changed little in two or three hundred years, but along the harbourside are the new, plain structures so necessary for the work of a busy port. There are amusement arcades too and all the popular accoutrements of a British seaside resort; these range from bingo to ice-cream via seafood stalls and souvenir shops.

Tucked around the corner, beyond the steep twisting climb known curiously as the Khyber Pass, is the Spa with its theatre and concert hall, while West Cliff echoes former, more genteel days with its Victorian arcades, hotels and well-kept gardens.

From the new bridge, the abbey appears to be in a precarious position because the cliff upon which it stands continues to shed huge lumps into the sea. Like so many of these coastal villages and towns, Whitby has long suffered from falling cliffs. On 24 December 1787 several houses slid into the sea below the abbey, as a result of which 196 families were made homeless over Christmas. Even as long ago as that, the landslide was thought to herald danger both to the abbey and to nearby St Mary's Church.

A similar event occurred on 15 December 1870, when a dozen houses were demolished, and local talk said this revealed bodies in their coffins in the cliff face above Henrietta Street. (The area around Henrietta Street used to be called 'Haggerlythe', a name I've heard in use today, but it was named Henrietta Street in 1761 in honour of the wife of Nathaniel Cholmley, who built the curious town hall in Church Street, the focus of a small market.) Subsequent minor falls lead to claims that skeletons can be seen in the bare cliff face, and one wonders whether this likelihood in any way influenced Bram Stoker in his use of the area for his Dracula novel, published in 1897.

There was a further landslip in 1923, when the cliff beyond the top of Henrietta Street was affected and revealed a seam of coal. Further minor slips have occurred, but none has caused such devastation as the 1787 disaster.

When I was a policeman in Whitby, my patrols at the foot of those cliffs beneath the abbey always made me wonder whether any of those landslides would repeat themselves in a major disaster. But the only memorable event in my service occurred when an off-duty fireman noticed a building with smoke pouring out and summoned all the local emergency services. They raced to the scene and located a small wooden building on Haggerlythe with dense, pungent fumes overwhelming it. But it was a false alarm. A local kipper merchant was smoking his herrings in the time-honoured way, with oak shavings. Kippers are one of Whitby's noted products, but only one man continues to cure them in that traditional way.

Leaving Whitby, the main road, now classified as the A171, continues to divide the dramatic coastline from the Moors. Permitting the Cleveland Way footpath to hug the coast, the road turns inland and passes through Hawsker after re-entering the National Park.

This calm village is noteworthy because of the fog horn which is located nearby. Its nickname is the 'Hawsker Bull', and its purpose is to warn shipping of the dangerous rocks along the shore line when the dense sea fogs descend. Danger points include Saltwick Nab and Black Nab, where there are many of these blanket coverings of thick, cold, clinging mist. Consequently, the loud, bull-like tones of the fog horn are a feature of life in this area, and it can be heard for miles, even through a curtain of thick sea mist.

At Hawsker is one of Yorkshire's many legendary links with Robin Hood. The story is that he and Little John came to Whitby Abbey where they were accommodated for a while. The fame of these heroes had preceded them, and the abbot and his monks requested a demonstration of their archery skills. The two outlaws were taken to the top of a tower in the abbey grounds and each was asked to shoot an arrow. Both arrows were discharged to the south-east and each landed on Whitby Laithes, a stretch of land near Hawsker, between Whitby and Robin Hood's Bay. It is said that the abbot was so delighted with these tremendously long shots that he ordered standing stones to be erected where the arrows fell. Robin's arrow was marked in Robin's Field, and John's in John's Field. The story loses a lot of credence when we realize the distance of the shots is around two miles. Nonetheless, there were several stone pillars in Hawsker. One was in a garden and another was found in a ditch in 1890 by the noted Whitby photographer Frank Meadow Sutcliffe. One had been removed by a farmer because it got in the way of his mowing machine, and it seems the other was later used in 1937 as a field roller on a Hawsker farm.

History also tells us that there used to be a stone shaft in Hawsker which marked the site of a cell built here by Asketil, a monk of Whitby Abbey, from whose name the village name is derived. Maybe one of those stones was that shaft?

South-east from Hawsker lies a large bay which faces almost due east. This is Robin Hood's Bay, which contains Fylingthorpe, Raw and the village of Robin Hood's Bay. This was described by the writer John Leyland in 1892 as 'one of the quaintest places imaginable, it hangs in picturesque confusion on the steep sides of a narrow gulley; it is yet another of these North Yorkshire fishing villages which clings to the cliffs and whose houses continue to drop into the sea'.

And so they do. In spite of formidable protection in the form of tall concrete sea-walls, the cliffs continue to be washed into the sea, leaving even modern bungalows, houses and the car-park precariously balanced on top. The village literally sits on the edge of the sea beneath the cliff. The older houses crowd along the shoreline, although many have been washed away; these older dwellings cling to the cliff in a most remarkable manner, and the village packs an enormous amount into a very small space. Narrow passages twist and turn between the cottages, and there is a dramatic walk-way along the modern but ugly sea-wall. These clustered homes led one lady travel writer to declare that it was 'the strangest village it has been my fortune to behold', and Arthur Mee said it was one of the most astonishing sights of the Yorkshire coast. Indeed, high tide actually flows up the village street, and one story tells of a ship's bowsprit smashing the window of a local inn. Where cars would normally park at the foot of the main street, there are cobles and fishing nets, and at high tide the sea splashes onto the double yellow 'No Parking' lines!

The village has been variously known as Bay Town or Robin Hood's Town, but today both the village and the surrounding countryside have become known as Robin Hood's Bay. They are really components of Fylingthorpe, whose sombre backcloth is Fylingdales Moor, home of the Ballistic Missile Early Warning Station. 'Fylingthorpe' means the 'settlement of Fygela', which bears no relationship to Robin Hood.

Indeed, the relationship between this area and Robin Hood is very tenuous. The story of Robin Hood is too well known to repeat here, save to remind ourselves that he was a noted outlaw who occupied a good deal of his time in dispute with the Sheriff of Nottingham, and history shows that a Robert Hode failed to appear at York Assizes in 1225, upon which he was declared an outlaw.

Robin Hood's exploits around Nottingham and South Yorkshire have produced many legends, some of which assert that, when his pursuers were too close, he fled north to the safety of the North York Moors around Whitby. He found a quiet bay on the edge of the Moors and decided this would be an ideal retreat. To this place he returned time and time again, and there he kept a small fleet of boats in constant readiness in case he was followed. He came most summers and spent time fishing, under the name of Simon Wise, but if he ever felt threatened, he would put to sea and remain afloat for several days until his hunters disappeared.

He kept his own men in peak condition by training them on archery butts built specifically for that purpose. One story says Robin himself shot an arrow from Stoupe Brow, a lofty piece of land a mile or so out of the village, and that it landed in the place now occupied by Robin Hood's Bay. Those butts are still called Robin Hood's Butts even though they are really ancient burial mounds. If indeed Robin ever came here, they would have provided a useful training ground, but the link between the outlaw and the village which bears his name is strained when we learn the village got its name around 1544. This was over three centuries after his supposed death at Kirklees, near Leeds.

As at other villages along this coast, the sea and tourism are the important sources of income. There is always the scent of the sea and fish, and the cry of wheeling gulls. The villagers used to augment their income by smuggling, sometimes making use of Boggle Hole as a landing place, while now they attend to the needs of visitors. Artists have settled here, and during the summer months the village is a busy, bustling place where visitors' cars are now banned.

There are two outmost points of the Bay, one known as the North Cheek (or Ness Point) and the other called South Cheek (or Old Peak). Because this was often called merely 'The Peak', it was frequently confused with Derbyshire's Peak District, so that name has been abandoned in preference for 'South Cheek'.

Beach walks and cliff treks head towards the Old Peak and Ravenscar, with the Cleveland Way utilizing some of this route. Walks along the beach can be dangerous due to the fast-rising tides and should be undertaken only as the tide is ebbing. Even so, a limited time is available. Bathing is dangerous too, but for sheer splendour this stretch of coastline is unrivalled. In places, the heather grows even to the edge of the cliff.

From Raven Hall Hotel, the climb down the Cheek cliff to the rock-strewn beach is worth every ache and pained breath. There can be few better coastal climbs. There are wide views of Robin Hood's Bay with red-roofed cottages dotted along the cliffs, while the cliffs at sea-level are continually shedding tiny flakes of shale. It tumbles endlessly like tiny pebbles to form soft heaps below, giving the rocky beach a curious black tint.

The area is now called Ravenscar. These cliffs rise to some 585 feet and once produced alum, while tradition says the Danes hoisted a flag here which bore a raven's image. One story says their leader was Ubba, who landed in either 866 or 867 and later sacked Whitby Abbey. The image of the raven dominates this sprawling collection of houses and farms.

But there were earlier visitors. The Romans built a fort in either the third or fourth century, its purpose being to observe and protect the coastline. Evidence of its presence came to light in 1774 when building started on Ravenshill Hall. This is now the Raven Hall Hotel, with its mock battlements overlooking the sea and a golf-course laid along the sloping cliffs. The ever-present sea breeze must play havoc with the game! Here, a stone was unearthed which bore the Latin inscription, 'Justinianus the Commander, prefect of the soldiers, built the fort with excellent augury.' Justinianus is thought to be the same man who left Britain for Gaul in AD 407, and this stone is now in Whitby Museum.

Ravenscar should not be confused with Ravenser, which occupied a site near the mouth of the Humber. Ravenser no longer exists, because in the fourteenth century it vanished due to coast erosion, but Shakespeare mentions it in *Richard III*.

South of Ravenscar is Beast Cliff, once called Bees Cliff or Darn Cliff. It is rich with springs, where bygone sailors would fill their casks from a waterfall known as the Watersplash, which fell over the cliffs into the sea. The isolated nature of this stretch of coastline makes it popular with nature lovers, when once it was popular with smugglers. Rumours say that treasure is buried below Beast Cliff.

A mile or so inland is the spreading hamlet of Staintondale, with the bulk of Hayburn Wyke in the distance. Staintondale stands in the middle of land once regarded as waste and little better than a desert. No one wanted its barren acres, and it was severely neglected until, in the twelfth century, King Stephen gave it to the Knights Hospitallers. This was upon condition that they built a church for him, and they were also charged with the duty of looking after poor people and travellers. They had to equip themselves with a loud horn and a bell, which had to be sounded each evening at twilight so that travellers might hear them and avail themselves of the hospitality on offer. The site of their bell tower is variously described as Bell Hill or Tofta Farm, both nearby. Because of this ancient order, the villagers once claimed exemption from tithes, tolls and land taxes, and also from jury service at quarter sessions and assizes. It became customary for the parish overseer to read this charter to the judge of assize if anyone from Staintondale was called to serve.

Today Staintondale remains a noted fox-hunting village whose hounds are trained to seek the unique cliff fox which has lived here for centuries. It is here that the sheer, lofty cliffs are noteworthy, for they are heavily covered in deciduous trees and make ideal cover for these foxes.

Hayburn Wyke, towering above the sea and surrounding landscape, dominates a peaceful cove which has considerable charm. Here the cliffs crumble and pretty streams join at Waters Meet, and there are wooden steps and a footbridge over the water. Like the neighbouring cliffs, these are noted for their profusion of trees. Oak, ash, hazel, chestnuts, walnut and thick undergrowth abound, which means there is a lot to interest the naturalist and even the geologist.

On the cliffs above, there used to be an old village, but a farm now occupies the site which now lies within a coniferous forest. Some of the narrow roads have breathtaking hills, corners and bridges masked by tall hedges and thickly wooded slopes.

Towards Scarborough, as Cloughton is approached, the boundary of the National Park slices across the A171 and effectively marks the southern tip of the coastal stretch of the Moors. Just beyond are the commuter villages of Scalby and Cloughton, now suburbs of Scarborough.

It was J.S. Fletcher in his volumes about *Picturesque Yorkshire* who said, 'There is only one way of seeing the full beauties and glories of Scarborough to perfection, and that is by first setting eyes on them from the sea.'

That is something we cannot do from the heathery heights of the Moors.

7

From Esklets to the Sea

> There is not in the wide world a valley so sweet,
> As that vale in whose bosom the bright waters meet.
>
> Thomas Moore (1779–1852)

There are more than one hundred dales within the North York Moors. They range from tiny valleys to fairly large ones, and most of them have names, although not every one appears on the Ordnance Survey tourist map.

The valleys of Yorkshire and other parts of the north have long been known as 'dales', a word derived from various sources including Old Saxon and Old Norse. Its pronunciation varies but in the North York Moors it is generally heard as 'deeal' or merely 'dle', as in Wyddle. For example. 'Farndale' can become either 'Farndle' or 'Farndeeal'.

The lovely dales within the North York Moors should not be confused with that portion of the county of North Yorkshire known as 'The Yorkshire Dales' or, merely, 'The Dales'. That term embraces an area on the eastern slopes of the Pennines and includes huge dales like Swaledale, Airedale, Wensleydale, Wharfedale and Nidderdale. Our moorland dales are a considerable distance from those, but they are equally entrancing – if not more so.

The name 'dale' is used for villages as well as valleys, and an example is the village of Glaisdale. This has a dale named after it (Glaisdale Dale), which in turn is a branch of a larger dale,

Eskdale. This is an example of how one larger dale (Eskdale) can have many smaller ones branching from it, and those small ones in turn have tinier ones leading off.

These smaller dales have produced their own terminology. The closed end is called its head; there are many Dale Head Farms within the Moors, and Rosedale boasts two of this name! The mouth of a dale is called the end, and so we have locations such as Danby End, Glaisdale End and Fryup End. Some very small dales or hollows are called slacks, such as Gelderslack and Wild Slack. In addition, some of the high moorland ridges between the dales are called riggs, and the points where they terminate in a dale are known as nabs or nab ends. The moorland streams which flow down most of the dales are known as becks, gills or ghylls. Where a track crosses a stream, the term 'wath' is used, and so we have localities like Slape Wath, Cow Wath, Hob Hole Wath, Blue Wath and many more.

Some of these dales contain isolated dwellings and farms which are collectively known by the name of the dale, for example Farndale. There is no village called Farndale, its two main collections of houses being Low Mill and Church Houses. Each is too small to be classified as a village.

Eskdale is the largest of the dales within the Moors National Park and differs from the others because it stretches from west to east. The River Esk, a premier salmon river, flows in that direction and enters the North Sea at Whitby, while all its main tributaries flow from south to north.

Most other rivers flow to the south and pour their waters into Ryedale, the exception being the River Derwent and its tributaries. The Derwent rises on Fylingdales Moor, and one would expect it to head straight for the nearby sea. But it doesn't. It meanders south through exquisite countryside and for some unaccountable reason turns inland and flows west beyond the boundaries of the National Park until, near Low Marishes south of Pickering, it joins the Rye at Rye Mouth. As the Derwent, it continues through Yorkshire and Humberside to flow into the River Ouse near Selby.

There is no doubt that all these moorland dales are beautiful, and their people are of a sturdy breed who carve a tough living from the landscape around them. They have cultivated the fertile floors of their dales where livestock farming is a major

Hunt House, a moorland farm near Goathland

The Moors Centre at Danby Lodge in Eskdale. This was formerly known as the North York Moors National Park Information Centre

Wheeldale Youth Hostel, 1982, once a shooting lodge belonging to the Crown

Roseberry Topping rises to 1,051 feet. The summit straddles the boundaries between the counties of North Yorkshire and Cleveland

Hutton-le-Hole, one of Yorkshire's prettiest villages and home of the Ryedale Folk Museum

The massive gooseberry which won the World Championship in 1952 at Egton Bridge Old Gooseberry Society Show

The Hole of Horcum

Opposite:
Mallyan Spout
tumbling into the
Murk Esk

Banniscue and Easterside, near Hawnby

Sutton Bank and Lake Gormire

HM The Queen's Ascot landau drawn by Cleveland Bays, 1963

The track of the North York Moors Railway across the Newton Dale

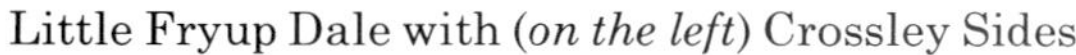

Little Fryup Dale with (*on the left*) Crossley Sides

Eskdaleside. A view of the Esk valley which stretches from the moors to the North Sea at Whitby

Danby-in-Cleveland, a rugged village in upper Eskdale

industry, comprising cattle and pigs for fattening, dairy produce or rearing. Cereals and root crops are widely produced, and in some cases the moor itself provides sustenance, in sheep-rearing for example, or game-keeping and the growth of coniferous trees for timber.

Most of the villages are self-contained in that they have their own shops and post offices, with access to the nearby market towns for other commodities. The motor car has given increased mobility to the dales people, for many of these isolated areas do not boast either a bus service or a railway station.

Ancillary services like those of the doctor, policeman and vicar are often shared, and many villages contain cottages which are let during the summer for holidays or as weekend homes. Whether this is good for the villages is open to debate – one argument is that it makes use of cottages which would otherwise remain empty and subsequently decay, and that the arrival of the weekenders does bring some commercial benefit to a village. A counter argument is that the purchase of these properties by wealthy outsiders denies young dalespeople a home of their own, for these cottages, many of which would be suitable for young couples born and bred in the area, are placed beyond their reach by high prices, and then used only sporadically.

It is an argument which will continue for many years, just as the arrival of outsiders can cause problems. Many fall in love with the wild, romantic views of summer and tumble into the trap of thinking that every day in the life of a moorland person is like one glorious, relaxed day in the life of a summer visitor. But it is not. It needs a special breed of human being to make a happy, fruitful life in the remoteness of those moorland dales – they are by no means commuterland and are not for urban man.

As a child and a young man, I could never understand why the Moors did not attract the same interest as, say, the Lake District, the Fens or the West Country. I quickly learned there were two main reasons: (1) that the North York Moors were sufficiently remote to deter all but the most dedicated of visitors, a fact which still applies because they are a substantial distance from any city, large conurbation or motorway and (2) when most of the early guidebooks were written, the dales in this area were sullied by the aftermath of a short burst of industrial activity. This faded in the early years of this century but its legacy remained a long time and perhaps deterred many visitors.

Now, the secret beauty of these dales and their villages has been leaked by the tourist organizations. This has added a new dimension and a new source of revenue to the moors – tourism. Although the Moors can still claim to be undiscovered as a major tourist area, visitors are increasing as these beauties are revealed.

Having generalized in this manner, I will take a closer look at some premier dales, but before examining the topography, it should be recorded that this area of the Cleveland Hills has produced a lovely breed of horse known as the Cleveland Bay.

These beautiful chestnut-brown animals with their jet-black manes and tails are known for their speed and stamina and for this reason are in demand for drawing state coaches and for driving contests as well as for riding, show-jumping, hunting or even working on a farm. There is no more versatile horse.

Their temperament makes them ideal for ceremonial occasions, and so Cleveland Bays draw the Queen's coach and they take part in many state occasions. The Queen keeps a string of Cleveland Bays, and such is their renown that the Cleveland Bay Horse Society exists to perpetuate the breed. In 1984, the centenary year of the Society, HM the Queen was President and gave a reception at Windsor Castle in honour of the Cleveland Bay.

Their origin lies here in the Cleveland Hills, where they were once known as Chapman Horses. A 'chapman' was a tinker, and these animals would carry his load of pots and pans from village to village. Broad-backed and sure-footed, the Chapman was also used as a farm working horse, where it was capable of pulling a plough or drawing a loaded cart, but because of its ability to keep its feet on the rough roads of yesteryear, it also found itself in demand for hauling stage coaches. As coaches were becoming faster on better roads, some Chapman horses were crossed with the best racing horses of the day to produce the Cleveland Bay. An early introduction of the small Yorkshire 'gallower' into the breed has produced a powerful horse without the appearance of a heavy carthorse but at the same time possessing its strength and stamina.

The pure Cleveland Bay has been described as the most beautiful breed of coaching horse the world has ever seen, and it continues to be bred in the Moors.

There are many boasts about this animal – one claim is that a Cleveland Bay carried seven hundred pounds for sixty miles in twenty-four hours, four times a week, something no other animal can do. The camel and the elephant could carry the load but lack the speed. Another Cleveland Bay carried at the trot a load of sixteen stones for sixteen miles and completed the journey within an hour.

Many inn signs bear illustrations of the Bay Horse, but few, if any, accurately depict the Cleveland Bay. Many portray horses with short tails, whereas the genuine Cleveland Bay has a long tail.

The Cleveland Bay is still bred in Eskdale, whose river rises at Esklets. This is a lovely name for a hollow in the moors between Westerdale and Farndale, and the infant Esk is joined by other becks as it meanders along the floor of Westerdale. Before arriving at Castleton, it is swollen by Baysdale Beck and Sleddale Beck.

Baysdale used to contain a Cistercian nunnery, and it is not surprising that this dale, and its nunnery, were noted for their solitude.

Sleddale Beck brings its waters from the Moors above Great Ayton and Guisborough by way of Commondale. Once an ugly collection of houses, among steep hills, Commondale village was the home of a brickworks, and as the industry declined, it became a haven of derelict buildings with rusting reminders of its brief industrial past. Some of these relics remained until the 1950s, but happily the village has now redeemed itself. It stands proud on its moorland hillside and copes with a steady stream of visitors heading from Teesside into Eskdale. In some ways, it is repeating an ancient role, for it was once at the meeting-place of several moorland tracks, including the Monks' Causeway which ran from Whitby Abbey to Guisborough Priory. Local legend says Captain Cook used this to walk from Great Ayton to Whitby via Glaisdale.

Downstream is Castleton, once the site of an ancient castle. This was a Norman structure of wood with three water moats at different levels, but its importance dwindled when it was superseded by Danby Castle two miles down the dale. Castleton, however, retained a position of importance in its own right, being the largest village in upper Eskdale. Its dark stone buildings with their blue slates typify Yorkshire strength and durability, and it was once a centre of local industry. There was a market here until the middle years of this century, and a disused weavers' mill near the station is a reminder of a busy past. The pub in the main street perpetuates the link, however tenuous, between the North York Moors and Robin Hood, for it is called 'The Robin Hood and Little John'. Its sign reads:

King gentlemen and yeomen good,
Call in and drink with Robin Hood,
If Robin be not at home,
Step in and drink with Little John.

Danby should really be called Danby End because it lies at the mouth of Danby Dale. It retains links with the past in its ancient Court Leet and Baron, which continues to administer matters like rights of way and parking upon common land within the parish. Across the Moors at Spaunton in Ryedale is another relic of these feudal courts. This is the Manor of Spaunton Court Leet and Court Baron with View of Frankpledge, whose duties include the taking of presentments with respect to matters of local concern, and the control and management of various common rights over Spaunton Moor.

Two other Courts Leet remain within the Moors, the Manor of Whitby Laithes Court Leet and the Manor of Fyling Court Leet, both of which manage local commons. There is a fifth at Clifton, near York.

In 1977 many of England's ancient courts had their jurisdiction curtailed, but the five mentioned above were retained to carry out their local functions. Out of thirty-one manorial courts in England and Wales, five are in North Yorkshire, and four of those are in a small area of the North York Moors. And they take their duties very seriously indeed. The Spaunton Court Leet barricaded a farmer's road with barbed wire when he refused to pay a fine of 85 pence which the court had imposed, and on another occasion threatened to fine the County Council if it erected 'No Parking' signs in Hutton-le-Hole.

Beyond Danby lies Danby Dale, with Castleton at its western end and Ainthorpe on the east. It runs south from Eskdale and penetrates three miles or so into the central block of the moors. Halfway along the dale stands St Hilda's Church, making Danby unusual because its church is at least a mile and a half from the village. With a fifteenth-century tower, it is built on the site of a previous chapel. Its vicarage was the home of Canon J.C. Atkinson, author of the classic *Forty Years on a Moorland Parish*, a remarkable volume which chronicled the life, times, superstitions, folklore and dialect of the area, together with antiquities of wider interest. In addition Canon Atkinson wrote other works and excavated many barrows on the moors, donating some of his discoveries to the British Museum. He died in 1900, but his name lives on as part of the moorland lore and he is buried in his beloved churchyard.

Higher in the dale is Botton Hall. Since 1955 it has housed a community of mentally and physically handicapped people who maintain themselves by making high-quality goods. In addition, they run the farms and their own village community, with its post office, shops and workshops, social centre and coffee bar. They are aided by volunteer staff but the emphasis is upon self-sufficiency, and the project is one of several established by the Camphill Village Trust, both in the UK and overseas.

Downstream from Danby is Ducks Bridge, the name probably being a corruption of 'Dux Bridge', meaning 'Duke's Bridge'. A single-span, narrow-arched bridge, it was built around 1386 to carry visitors across the Esk to Danby Castle.

Snug in the valley below the Beacon Hill is the hamlet of Houlsyke. This is one of the least intrusive of the Eskdale villages but surprisingly, less than a century ago, it was a thriving business centre. Eskdale was then noted as a pig-rearing district whose nerve-centre was Houlsyke. Pigs were killed and cured before being taken by horse-drawn wagons to Whitby for shipping to London. There was also a brisk trade in sheep and wool, and the centre of all this was a public house called the Fat Ox, now an ordinary house.

Near Houlsyke, the road divides. One arm leads to Lealholm and the other diverts into Fryup.

Fryup is a scattered community of sturdy houses and farms spread across two dales, Little Fryup Dale and Great Fryup Dale. Fryup's odd name causes both amusement and speculation, and it may be derived from Friga, an old English personal, name, while 'up' or 'hop' means a small valley. Little Fryup Dale is indeed a small but exquisite valley.

Here, on Crossley Sides, almost in the shadow of Danby Castle, as a child I picked bilberries by the basketload. These small dark blue berries with the delightful bloom grow wild on many parts of the moor and are variously known as whortleberries, blueberries, blaeberries, blackberries, cowberries, whinberries, heatherberries, wineberries, mulberries and by many other names. They are found on the undersides of a small, shrub-like plant which grows among the heather, and although they are troublesome to collect, they are worth the effort. Bilberry pie with cream is delicious, and so are other local dishes made from them.

Fryup's two dales are divided by an elevated piece of moor, the southern tip of which is called Fairy Cross Plain. This name goes back almost two centuries, the 'cross' element coming from a point where two tracks merged and 'fairy' reminding us that this was thought to be the haunt of fairies.

Fairy rings, natural circles on the ground caused by the Fairy Ring Fungus, were accepted as magical, and children would play around them, taking care never to run nine times around any one ring. If they did, it was understood the fairies would acquire power over them.

Today, we smile at these beliefs which were common even during the early part of this century, but these folk took their superstitions seriously. One example involves an old lady who claimed she saw a fairy on Fairy Cross Plain. He came down the hill towards the beck and was described as a little green man with a queer sort of cap. She said he and his companions 'used to come down the hill by this deear [door] and gaed in at yon brig-steean'. She meant they used to go into the ground near the stone which supported the bridge and where there was a culvert. When her husband queried this, she retorted that the mole lives underground, so why shouldn't a fairy?

Another belief was that these fairies made butter, for the sound of their work could often be heard at night. It was rather like the noise of the fairies of Kettleness doing their washing, for the sound of the latters' bittles must have been similar to that of the slap of buttermaking. It seems that, when they made it, they smeared it all over the lady's cottage gate!

Yet another tale accounts for the finding of a fairy child in a hayfield. In the lady's words, these are the circumstances: 'It was liggin' in a swathe of the half-made hay, as bonny a lahtle thing as ever yan seen. But it was a fairy-bairn, it was quite good to tell. But it did not stay lang wi' t'lass at fun it. It a soort o' dwinied away and she aimed the fairy-mother couldn't deea wivoot it any langer.' This is North Riding dialect, and the words mean, 'It was lying in a swathe of half-made hay, as pretty a little thing as anyone ever saw. But it did not stay long with the girl who found it. It sort of withered away, and she supposed the fairy-mother couldn't manage without it any longer.'

There were rumours too, of a troll living on the hill behind Fairy Cross Plain, and all these tales link up strongly with the hob or dwarf tales which are such a feature of moorland folklore.

At the end of Great Fryup Dale, the Esk broadens before tumbling through the picturesque ravine called Crunkley Gill on its route to Lealholm. Crunkley Gill, shaded and overgrown as the river crashes over rocks, was once owned by Orm, the man who bought Kirkdale Minster. It is said to be the biggest rock garden in England, for there is a profusion of plants here, including some rare ones. As the Esk enters Lealholm, it reduces speed, and this once quiet village, with its spacious green surrounded by cottages, is now a tourists' mecca. Toilets, a car-park and additional shops have suddenly appeared where none existed in my youth. Its attractions include the wide, slow-moving river, the stepping-stones and the towering Lealholm Bank with stupendous views from the top. A foreign correspondent, accustomed to seeing many other countries, wrote of this part of the Moors, 'They differ from all others I have ever seen, and in this particular – that elsewhere you have to go in search of beautiful views; here, they come and offer themselves to be looked at.'

Half way up Lealholm Bank is a modern Catholic church, and almost opposite is an older Anglican church with the tiniest of towers, only some six feet wide at the base.

This long climb leads high onto the Moors to cross the A171 and continue into Ugthorpe. This means 'Uggi's village', but it is noted for its strong links with Father Nicholas Postgate, the eighty-two-year-old Roman Catholic priest martyred at York for ministering to his parishioners. It was one of the few villages to maintain a resident Catholic priest throughout the Reformation and the penal times, and priests' hiding-places have been found in some of Ugthorpe's older buildings. Its present Catholic church was not opened until 1857 and is dedicated to St Anne. It was officially opened by Cardinal Nicholas Wiseman, the first Archbishop of Westminster, and almost opposite is the Anglican church, opened in the same year.

Two miles downstream is Glaisdale, of which an earlier guide said, 'There is no air more vigorating, the spot has many natural charms. It is among meandering streams and wooded vales, and around for miles are the beautiful moors.' Arthur Mee later described it as a 'dale shut off from the world by the moors'. Descriptions of this kind give it a romantic and pleasurable image, and indeed it was the first twenty-two years of my life in this village that nurtured my love of the countryside and my interest in matters like the dialect, folklore, superstitions and customs of the district.

It is one of North Yorkshire's focal points for folklore, tradition and romance. The folklore aspect is dealt with in Chapter 9 when I discuss the hob which lived hereabouts, and the romance comes in the shape of Beggar's Bridge, still very much in evidence as its graceful arch spans the Esk near the railway station.

According to legend, it was built by Tom Ferris, whose initials are carved on a stone on the parapet, along with the date 1619. (There are several spellings of his name, including Firris, Ferries and Ferrers, but I will stick to the one I've known since I was born.) Tom was a local man of modest means who fell in love with Agnes Richardson, the daughter of a well-to-do farmer from Egton. He had to cross the Esk each time he wished to meet her, always a difficult task, and more so when the river was in flood. An added problem was that Agnes's father did not approve and did his best to end the relationship, probably due to Tom's lack of prospects. The pair had to meet in secret, and Tom quickly realized that, if he was to win her hand in marriage, he had to make some money. Because he liked the idea of travelling, he left Glaisdale and joined a ship at Whitby. He found himself fighting against the Spanish Armada, after which he was involved in looting some Spanish galleons, and he returned to become Mayor of Hull and Warden of its Trinity House. He had made good, and so he built his famous bridge and married Agnes.

That's what the story says, and who wants to spoil a good romantic yarn?

His sturdy bridge survived the disastrous floods of 1930, and it remains to this day. But there is one problem – it is in need of repairs, and the question of ownership and responsibility has also arisen. Its charms are almost concealed between two modern structures, two bridges of iron, one carrying the road to the foot of the notorious Limber Hill with its gradient of one in three (thirty-three per cent), and the other carrying the railway towards Whitby.

But Glaisdale has not always been gentle and romantic. Once it was a busy iron-ore village where even the local inn, owned by my grandfather, Thomas Rhea, had the unglamorous name of the Three Blast Furnaces. It overlooks the scene of Glaisdale's former iron-ore workings and had changed its name *from* the Anglers' Rest; grandfather changed it back again, to the name it still enjoys. Those three blast furnaces and the accompanying works disappeared long ago, and grandfather bought the site. The inn remains one of three in the village.

Glaisdale's short but important role in the iron-ore boom did much to establish Middlesbrough as a major steel-producing town. Its works operated between 1866 and 1876, as did others at nearby Grosmont and its adjoining hamlet, confusingly known as Esk Valley. (The hamlet of Esk Valley, which had an ironstone mine between 1860 and 1877, lies within the valley known as Esk Valley!)

In addition to the Anglers' Rest, Glaisdale bears other visible reminders of the iron-ore boom. One is 'The Grange', once the home of the local ironmaster and now overlooking the cricket field and the former site of the blast furnaces. A further relic is the planned route of a railway line which was never completed. As children, we all knew it as the Paddy Waddell Railway. Mr John Waddell, with teams of Irish workmen, began to build a line from Glaisdale to carry iron ore over the moors. It was going to be called the Cleveland Mineral Extension Railway, linking Lingdale with Glaisdale, and the project began in 1873, but it suffered a series of mishaps and was never completed. Some cuttings, sidings and bridges were constructed, and even a Railway Hotel was built at Moorsholm. One cutting, now filled with marshy plants, can be seen near Liverton Road End on the

Whitby–Guisborough road, and a stone bridge over the empty line marks its proposed links with the existing Eskdale line near Glaisdale.

Running south-west from Glaisdale village is the dale, pushing almost three miles into the Moors. The weaving of cloth was a small industry here in the sixteenth and seventeenth centuries, and at its end stands St Thomas's Anglican church. This administers a legacy from Tom Ferris, builder of Beggar's Bridge, and is within sight of Hart Hall Farm, haunt of the legendary hob.

Another link with the ancient past is found in the Glaisdale and Lealholm Association for the Prosecution of Felons.

In the Middle Ages, societies of this kind existed to assist the parish constable to control local crime and were created when the villagers formed themselves into associations for self-protection. They built up their finances through rewards for the recovery of stolen livestock. As the modern police service gained acceptance and village policemen served in rural areas, these societies disappeared. But the one at Glaisdale remains, and it is believed to be the only one in England.

Meetings are still held but no one seems to know when it last brought a criminal to justice. When the law abolished the distinction between felonies and misdemeanours in 1978, it effectively rendered the term 'felon' obsolete, and there were fears that this society would disappear. But it didn't. It still functions, and there are fringe benefits for members such as a funeral club and expenses for jury service. But the only current official function of this Association is to organize its annual dinner.

Two miles down the Esk from Glaisdale is Egton Bridge, with its twin village of Egton on the hill overlooking the valley. The name comes from 'Egetune', meaning 'town of oaks'. In 1070 the villages were given to Nigel Fossard by William the Conqueror. The place was so delightful even then that the Conqueror's blacksmith left him at York in order to settle in Egton!

Egton Bridge is one of Yorkshire's most beautiful villages, and it occupies an idyllic site on the River Esk. It is a famous Roman Catholic parish whose adherence to the faith caused it to be name 'the village missed by the Reformation', and it is the birthplace of the martyr Nicholas Postgate. Evidence of that staunch faith is seen in the massive Catholic church of St Hedda, more fitting for a large city than for a tiny moorland village. The great roof is ribbed and painted blue with golden stars, while the Belgian terracotta work of the altar makes it more like a Continental edifice than a sober English place of worship. It is a marvellous tribute to Postgate's work, and an annual Mass is held in his honour either here or at Ugthorpe.

Halfway up the hill between Egton and Egton Bridge is the Mass House (see pages 55–7) which from 1952 until going to press was occupied by Mr Tom Ventress, former World Champion Gooseberry Grower. He once grew a berry thirty drams eight grains, but in 1982 this was beaten by Bob Bennison, whose berry was heavier by one grain.

The Egton Bridge Old Gooseberry Society was formed in 1800, and the Society holds an annual show in the village on the first Tuesday in August. It is one of only two such shows in England and here monster gooseberries are displayed in all their colours and varieties – each is around the size of a hen's egg, and the secrets of growing such beauties are closely guarded.

Up the hill, Egton's church of St Hilda is now Anglican, and it occupies a commanding site close to the Mass House; the original was built in 1349 but this was re-built in the nineteenth century in the Norman style. Its almsbox is made from timber out of Nelson's flagship, and the area around the church was once said to be haunted by a bargest, a type of bier ghost described as neither animal nor human. It was thought to foretell death.

Egton has made its mark, for it hosts one of the largest agricultural shows in the region, a mammoth undertaking for such a small community.

It was at Egton in the thirteenth century that the estate owners, the de Mauleys, obtained a market charter which permitted an annual fair of eight days duration. A further charter providing for the holding of four further fairs was granted by William III, and these became the famous Hiring Fairs of the area, held at various times, a popular time being the Feast of St Martin, or Martinmas Day, although others occurred in May, at Whitsuntide and on Michaelmas Day. They were of a week's duration and an occasion for holiday fun, the only holiday in the year for farm workers. They were also the time when farmers took on hired labour. Hopeful labourers and domestic servants would gather at the hiring fairs where they were examined by prospective bosses. Terms were discussed by both parties, and the quality of the food was important too because the staff 'lived in'. Word soon got around if a particular place was a 'bad meat house' or if the missus was rude or overbearing. When the deal was struck, it was sealed by the boss passing over a God's Penny, sometimes called a fastning penny, a coin which legally sealed the bargain and ensured that the labourer worked for that man over the next fifty-one weeks. (That coin could be a penny, but it was usually a shilling, rising to a half-crown and then five shillings around the time of World War I. In spite of its face value, the coin was always known as either God's Penny or the fastning penny.) New workers started at the end of the fair and could return the following year if they wished to find a new boss, or if the boss wished to find a new worker.

The Hiring Fairs are still remembered but ended with the passing of the Agricultural Wages Act of 1924.

Out of these early fairs has grown the annual show of the Egton Horse and Agricultural Society. Founded in 1876, the Society's show takes place in August and is now one of the major country shows of the district.

Situated at the junction of two railway lines and two rivers, Grosmont occupies a strategic position. One of the railway lines is the Whitby-Middlesbrough British Rail route, and the other is the privately owned North York Moors Railway, meeting at the Grosmont railway station. The Moors Railway uses a route constructed by George Stephenson and officially opened in May 1836. It was then a horse-drawn service, but in 1845 George Hudson of York introduced a steam locomotive. At one stage, the gradients were so steep that the coaches had to be hauled up the one-in-ten incline by rope, a fact noted by Dickens when he used it.

Two rivers meet at Grosmont too, the Esk and its main tributary, the Murk Esk. The latter flows down from the moors, starting its official journey at Beck Hole, and on occasions its waters are a deep rich brown colour, due not to mud but to peat deposits, and it is probably for this reason that the river is called Murk or Mirk Esk.

The district around modern Grosmont is beautiful and scenic, and yet within the very recent past it was a small industrial centre. When I passed daily by rail on my way to school at Whitby, the brickworks were in production and the village bore signs of its links with the iron-ore boom of the area. Today, few signs remain, even though this village was originally responsible for the rapid growth of Middlesbrough as a steel town.

Other names, like Rosedale, feature strongly in this brief industrial moment of the Moors' history, but the honour for starting the Klondike-style rush really belongs to Grosmont.

In 1836 a Mr Wilson of the Tyne Iron Company noticed an ironstone seam at Grosmont. It was five miles inland from the coastal seams which had hitherto supplied his requirements, and it was four feet six inches thick. Its exposure was accidental, for it had been revealed during the building of the Whitby-Pickering railway line. A mine was opened and some hundred thousand tons of ore per year were sent by the new railway line to Whitby for shipping to the Tyne. This mine closed in 1871.

This rich seam extended across the moors to Skinningrove on the coast. That village continues to be the location of a complex of works administered by British Steel, and it was here that the seam was found to be fourteen feet thick and of the very best quality. Thus this corner of Yorkshire became the source of the finest ironstone in the country, and Teesside flourished because of it.

On the northern slopes of Eskdale, above Sleights, is the quiet village of Aislaby, one of two in the North York moorland area bearing this name. The other is near Pickering.

The Eskdale Aislaby's name probably comes from the Danish meaning 'Asulf's farm', and it remains a snug backwater although the A171 passes nearby. Aislaby's quarries have given the village a place in history because they produce stone of great durability. Many piers along the English coast are supported with stone from here, and it was also used to build London Bridge. There is a possibility that it was used during the reconstruction of Whitby Abbey between 1148 and 1175 on the orders of Abbot Richard, who also built a chapel at Aislaby and dedicated it to St Margaret.

Sleights is a large and growing village which sprawls across the valley below Aislaby. It is a community of modern houses, some on the grand scale, and it reflects a recent well-to-do and rather genteel style of life. The name means 'flat land near water'.

Across the river here, above the railway station, is a striking bridge which carries the A169 almost past the edge of Sleights. It provides commanding views along the valley and above the lower reaches of the village, but this is not the first bridge. An attempt was made to build one around 1197, under instructions from the abbot of Whitby Abbey. The necessary stone was quarried nearby, probably at Aislaby, and the monks who were building it burned their own lime. In that year, 1197, a canon from Malton fell into the lime pit and was poisoned by the gases. Two bystanders went to his rescue, but they suffered the same fate.

Nearby, at Sleights Lane End, upon the side of the Whitby to Guisborough moor road, there is a commemorative plaque which records the first enemy aircraft shot down in England during World War II. It was a Heinkel bomber and fell close to this junction on 3 February 1940. The British pilot was Peter Townsend, later to be a Group Captain and known for his ill-fated romance with Her Royal Highness Princess Margaret, sister of Queen Elizabeth II.

Sleights certainly lacks the austere upland appearance of other moorland villages, although it lies at the foot of Blue Bank. This steep climb carries the A169 from Sleights towards Pickering and crosses heights rising some thousand feet above sea-level. Blue Bank was the first surfaced road in the Whitby district, being built in 1759 to link Whitby to Saltersgate via Sleights, and by 1788 there was a twice-a-week cart service along this route to link Whitby, Pickering and York.

At its foot is an Anglican church in the style of the thirteenth century, even though it was built in 1895. The nearby Catholic church is much more modern, but Sleights is the site of a very ancient chapel, about a mile and a half upstream. Tradition says the chapel is the setting of a scene in Sir Walter Scott's *Marmion*, and as long ago as 1762 it was described as a 'poor mean structure covered in thatch situated in a damp place near the River Esk'. The chapel is linked to one of Whitby's most ancient and curious customs, the Horngarth Ceremony, popularly known as 'the Planting of the Penny Hedge'.

On 16 October 1159, three local men were hunting wild boar. They were Ralph de Percy, who was Lord of Sneaton, William de Bruce, Lord of Ugglebarnby, and a member of the Allanson family. The boar took refuge in the chapel, which was occupied by a hermit monk, and the three hunters rushed in to kill it. But the terrified animal was given sanctuary by the monk. Because the monk sheltered it in one of his cells, the three men severely attacked him with their boar staves. He died later from his injuries. The story says that before he died, he was visited by the abbot of Whitby Abbey who said he intended to trace and punish these men. Even then, the hermit pleaded with him, asking that they be forgiven on condition that they and their successors paid a penance for their sins.

The penance he imposed was that, at sunrise on the eve of Ascension Day every year, these men or their successors should go to a wood on Eskdaleside and collect some short staves, the cost of which should not exceed one penny. They must carry them personally to Whitby and arrive before nine o'clock that same morning. At nine o'clock, they had to set the staves in the mud of the harbour and weave them in the form of a small barrier which must withstand at least three tides. If this flimsy hedge failed that test, all the lands of those men or their successors would be forfeited to the abbot of Whitby Abbey, or his successors. This became known as the Horngarth Ceremony.

For more than eight hundred years that hedge has been planted, and it has always withstood the prescribed three tides. Since 1948 the penance has been performed by members of the Hutton family.

The ancient penance did contain a release clause. It said that should the tide (or full sea, as it was written) ever prevent the planting of the hedge, the penance should cease. And not once in all those years did that occur – until 1981. As the little party comprising officials and members of the Hutton family, plus the inevitable sightseers, gathered to plant the hedge at 9 a.m. on Ascension Eve, 27 May 1981, the site was covered with eight feet of sea water. It was a freak tide, but it was sufficient to free the family from the penance of all those years. Instead of calling, 'Out on ye, out on ye, out on ye', the bailiff formally declared that the penance imposed in 1159 was now at an end. It marked the conclusion of Whitby's unique custom.

But it couldn't end like that! The Hutton family have decided to continue planting their Penny Hedge, but no longer under duress. If they fail in their self-imposed task, their lands will not now be forfeited to the successors of Whitby Abbey's authorities!

Two miles south of Sleights is the entrancing hamlet of Littlebeck, said by some to contain the sweetest woodland in all Eskdale. The access roads are very steep and very narrow, but the hamlet is worthy of the effort. It houses some lovely buildings, including the workshops of a woodcarver known as the Gnomeman because he carves a small gnome on every item.

One unpublicized custom is the annual Rose Queen ceremony which is still held in August, when a local girl is crowned Rose Queen and floated on the river on a raft. It is this same river in which John Reeves drowned himself. He was the man who revealed Father Postgate to the authorities in nearby Red Barns Farm at Ugglebarnby.

Above Littlebeck is a location known as Red Gates. Over the years, those gates, which are at the side of the B1416 from Ruswarp to Scarborough, have been all colours, but when I last called they were painted red! They lead into three tracks, one of which takes the visitor to Falling Foss, a lovely waterfall in a sylvan setting, always beautiful but at its most dramatic when in flood, as it cascades forty feet over a cliff. The surrounding rocks are thick with ferns, moss and woodland plants, and deep in the woods nearby is a sturdy house called Midge Hall. Also tucked away in the woods is a home carved out of solid rock, the work of George Chubb. He created it in 1780, and it even includes two carved stone armchairs. It will accommodate about twenty people.

It is worth venturing higher up this lovely valley to Maybeck, where, on the side of the hill, there is a house which was once the workshop of a clogmaker. He used elms from the nearby woods but ended his business about sixty years ago. The craft has since disappeared from this area.

Down in the valley is Ruswarp, whose houses have extended until they link with those of Whitby. Ruswarp, location of a thriving cattle mart, has little of ancient historic interest, although there has been a mill here since the time of the Domesday Book. It was then owned by Whitby Abbey, but the present flour mill was re-built in 1752 and again in 1946. It is one of the district's best-known landmarks, along with the 120-foot-high viaduct which crosses the valley to the Whitby side. This once carried the railway from Scarborough to Whitby's West Cliff station, now closed, and provides incredible views of the upper harbour.

Across the widening Esk at Ruswarp is a bridge rather like a miniature Sydney Harbour bridge. It was built in 1936 to replace an earlier one washed away by the terrible floods of 23 July 1930 which devastated the area; the Whitby lifeboat came upstream to Ruswarp to rescue people marooned on the roofs of their homes. Today, that same river above the dam is non-tidal and calm enough for summer boating upstream to Sleights. The Bridge Inn at the end of this graceful structure was once owned by one of my grandfathers, Jim Walker, and salmon can be seen leaping this dam.

Ruswarp also suffered during the bombardment of Whitby in December 1914, when German ships shelled the town and the abbey, and killed a coastguard in his clifftop station. Over two hundred shells were fired, some of which came as far inland as Ruswarp, and one even reached Sleights, four miles from the sea.

Beyond Ruswarp, the Esk widens as it meanders into the upper reaches of Whitby Harbour, its water having undertaken a beautiful journey from the heights of Westerdale Moor.

8

South into the Rye

'Meandering with a crazy motion through wood and dale.'
Samuel Taylor Coleridge (1772–1834)

The most southerly village in the North York Moors National Park is Coxwold, one of its most stylish and attractive. It is so full of interest and such a classic delight that one could spend time pleasurably discovering all its facets and absorbing its distinctive atmosphere.

That it stands on the edge of some of Yorkshire's most beautiful countryside is beyond dispute, albeit incidental, because the village itself is superbly appointed. In 1978 it won the Yorkshire Rural Community Council's Best Kept Village trophy, an indication of the pride the inhabitants have in their home.

Within a short distance along its wide main street can be found Shandy Hall, home of the eccentric humorist and author Laurence Sterne; a strikingly handsome parish church on a hilltop setting; the mellow Colville Hall; a lovely inn called the Fauconberg Arms; an old grammar school dating to 1603; a pottery where one can see products being created; some almshouses from the days of Charles II, and further along the road, at the foot of the village, just outside the National Park's boundaries, Newburgh Priory, wherein lies the body of Oliver Cromwell.

As if this is not enough, it lies in an exquisite rural setting which boasts other features like Byland Abbey, Kilburn, with its workshops of Mousey Thompson the noted woodcarver, the famous White Horse landmark, and Sutton Bank's lofty views.

It was to this rustic paradise that Laurence Sterne came as vicar in 1760 to live in the fifteenth-century house which he called Shandy Hall. He altered it to his own curious design, since when it has been restored and opened to the public on Wednesdays and at other times by appointment. There, one can almost feel the presence of this eccentric master of comic writing.

Sterne came to Coxwold from nearby Sutton-on-the-Forest, where he had written the first two parts of his classic novel *The Life and Times of Tristram Shandy, Gentleman*. This was finished at Coxwold, after which he wrote *A Sentimental Journey*. His writing was described as bawdy, witty and zestful, work of a kind hardly expected from a vicar. I like the line: 'I do not know what my father was about when he begat me', and admire his advice when he told parishioners that those who liked the vicar should face him in church, while those who did not might face the other way.

If the local people failed to understand their strange vicar, his writings now appeal to a worldwide readership, and many make Coxwold a place of literary pilgrimage. Shandy Hall is a gem and reveals much of the humour of this interesting man who wrote that he was 'as happy as a prince at Coxwold'.

Sterne died in London in 1768 and was buried at St George's Church, Hanover Square. Rumours suggested his remains were stolen by body-snatchers, and when a body was being dissected for anatomical research, it was thought to be that of Sterne. The top of its skull had already been removed, but orders were given for it to be re-interred. In 1969, when that London cemetery was being cleared, the Laurence Sterne Trust asked permission to transfer his remains to Coxwold. Five skulls and some bones were found in his supposed grave, but one skull had had its top sawn off. Expert assessment convinced the Trust that his true remains had been traced, and these were buried in Coxwold, almost within sight of Shandy Hall.

While Sterne arrived in Coxwold to a life of bucolic happiness,

Oliver Cromwell's arrival could not have been in greater contrast.

After Cromwell's body had been exhumed and hung minus its head at London's Tyburn, his third daughter, Mary, managed to get possession of the headless corpse. In 1657 she had married Thomas, the second Viscount Fauconberg, the Fauconbergs being owners of Newburgh Priory. Fearful of further horrors that might be perpetrated upon her father's body, she smuggled his remains to this North Yorkshire village. They were placed in a tomb and hidden in the roof, but when the roof was raised, the tomb was exposed. It can be seen by visitors, for this lovely house and gardens are occasionally open to the public.

But the nagging question remains – does this curious block of bricks really contain the body of Oliver Cromwell? It has never been opened, so no one really knows; there has been pressure upon the family to allow examination of the tomb, but all attempts have failed. Not even a royal visitor could compel the family to reveal the contents. When Edward VII visited Newburgh as Prince of Wales, he cunningly persuaded the estate's mason to break into the tomb, but the plotting pair were caught in the act and halted. It remains intact, and so does the mystery of its contents.

Thus Coxwold has two mystery bodies – are both Sterne and Cromwell buried here? Or neither of them?

Newburgh Priory, founded by the Augustinian friars in 1145, is worth a visit, if only to see its Water Garden.

This most southerly extension of the Moors National Park includes the sleepy village of Wass, which overlooks the splendours of Byland Abbey, and Ampleforth, whose main street is a mile long. This straggling village lies beneath the sheltering heights of the Moors, and the National Park boundary runs along the main street and so divides the village.

Ampleforth is noted for its modern abbey and college, which are dealt with on pages 57–9. The village history dates at least to 1086, when it was called 'Ampreforde', meaning 'the ford of the sorrel', and there used to be a village market outside the White Swan Inn. It has long been known as a place of liberty because there has never been a lord of the manor or a squire, and this was one of the reasons why Benedictine monks were able to settle nearby in 1803 to begin their present abbey. Even today, the village is the home of many self-employed tradesmen who continue the tradition of liberty and enterprise.

The Anglican parish church of St Hilda stands just off the main street and boasts a Norman font with a good deal of thirteenth-century work, including an unfinished carving of the signs of the zodiac. Its registers go back to 1690. The Catholic parish church of St Benedict in the village contains some early work by the Kilburn woodcarver Mousey Thompson; his first commission in oak was a cross for the War Memorial. It was sought by the then parish priest, Father Paul Nevill, who made such an impact as headmaster of Ampleforth College.

One curious relic of the past comes in the form of the Ampleforth Sword Dance, one of the few in Yorkshire to survive in its original form. It was revived by a monk of Ampleforth, and in fact a team from Ampleforth College performed it at the Royal Albert Hall in 1950.

An even older relic is above the village at Studfold Ring. This is probably the finest earthwork of its type in the district, but its purpose is not known. It may be the burial place for men who guarded the hills in the area, or it could have been a cattle enclosure.

To the immediate west of Ampleforth is Shallowdale, a lovely valley once occupied by Quakers who grew flax. The soft water of the beck was ideal for cleaning the flax, consequently Shallowdale became the focus of a very busy weaving industry. This declined until in 1834 there were only three weavers in Shallowdale, and it ended about twenty years later.

To the south of Ampleforth and neighbouring Oswaldkirk is the Gilling Gap, a broad, green and productive valley which forms an upper reach of Ryedale. It is into Ryedale that many moorland streams flow south from the moors. Some of these enter Ryedale through Bilsdale as they feed the River Seph which joins the Rye north of Rievaulx, having flowed almost the length of Bilsdale, a ranging, broad valley of very scattered farms and cottages. There is only one village along its fourteen miles or so, and this Chop Gate. It is a lofty place whose name is pronounced locally as 'Chop Yat'. 'Yat' is an old dialect word for 'gate' or 'way', and 'Chop' may come from the Scandinavian '*kaup*', meaning a pedlar or a chapman. It is feasible that in the Middle Ages 'Chop Gate' was derived from 'Chapman's Way', for the hills above the valley bore many tracks and routes. Some are a legacy of peak periods of activity around Rievaulx Abbey.

The village has a curiously modern village hall and spacious car-park, while halfway down the dale, near a bubbling stream, is the remote and beautiful church of St John designed by Temple Moor. It serves the whole dale and has a most unusual clock whose ponderous tick adds a melancholy tone to its moorland silence. That church stands almost opposite a rare green-painted telephone kiosk. It is at Fangdale Beck, and although it recently occupied this new site, it has managed to retain its distinctive colouring.

If this splendid dale has any claim to fame other than its rugged scenery, it is its ancient links with fox-hunting, witch-hares and William the Conqueror. An account of the witch-hares appears in Chapter 9. So far as fox-hunting is concerned, the Bilsdale Hounds are said to be one of the oldest packs in the country, founded in the seventeenth century by the Duke of Buckingham. (He is also thought to have founded the Sinnington Hunt not far away, which also claims to be Britain's oldest.) One story says that while hunting in Bilsdale, he fell at Tarn Hole and struck his head on a rock now known as the Buckingham Stone. He died later in Kirkbymoorside. Other stories claim he sat on the wet grass during a hunt and died two days later from a cold. The probable truth is that the Buckingham Stone is the burial place of one of the Duke's hunters. After an exhausting ride into Tarn Hole, where a fox was killed, the Duke's horse collapsed and died. The Duke ordered that the animal be buried where it fell and that a huge boulder be rolled over the grave in commemoration.

The headquarters of the Bilsdale Hunt was at Spout House, now the location of the Sun Inn which stands on the roadside. This isolated complex boasts a small country inn bearing the name Sun Inn, and alongside is a sixteenth-century thatched cruck house, once also called the Sun Inn. That lovely old thatched building, recently restored, ceased to be an inn in 1914, its last customers being soldiers on their way to fight in France. Its restoration was authorized by the North York Moors National Park Committee, and in May 1982 it was opened to the public. As each building is known as both Spout House and the Sun Inn, which name belongs to which building? Harry Mead, in his well-researched book *Inside the North York Moors*, reveals that neither is Spout House; that name belongs to a small cottage nearby, so it seems that both can call themselves the Sun Inn!

The landlord of the modern Sun Inn is William Ainsley; the inn has been in his family for nearly two hundred years, and the eldest son is always called William, who is by tradition landlord of the inn.

To the right of the inn's door, a tombstone stands close to the wall. It shows a fox's mask carrying a whip and hunting horn, and bears the inscription: 'In memory of Bobbie Dowson, died June 17, 1902, aged 86 years. Whip to Bilsdale Hounds for upwards of 60 years'. Because the vicar objected to this as a tombstone, it was left outside the churchyard for several years until the hunt followers positioned it outside Bobby's favourite inn.

Bobby Dowson's life epitomizes the hunting reputation of the valley in which he spent his life, and he claimed ancestors who had hunted with Buckingham. Indeed, Bobby was instrumental in keeping alive the Bilsdale Hunt, for at one stage he kept its only surviving hound. Born in 1816, he spent his entire life hunting; he never married and lived alone in a small cottage with a horse and a few cows. In the world of fox-hunting, his word was respected and no one argued with him. His knowledge of the fox was such that he could anticipate its movements, and he was reputed to have been at the kill every time. Even when he went off in the opposite direction to the fleeing fox, he would arrive at the kill in advance of the more affluent, mounted huntsmen. His appearance was typical of a fox-hunter – a small, wiry man with a pointed nose. He loved hunting and cricket, both of which centred around the Sun Inn, where he would sit and tell his stories.

It was Bobby, sitting in the Sun Inn, who told stories of the witch-hares, and I have a letter from Major J. Fairfax-Blakeborough, an author of the Moors, who knew Bobby and listened to his personal accounts of tales from more than a century and a half ago. These yarns show that fox-hunting in Bilsdale was almost a mania. There are tales of hunting in the dark, of grown men riding to the terror of young people, and of farmers at work in the fields grabbing horses without saddles or bridles in order to join a passing hunt. But perhaps the most illustrative is the tale of a parson, the Reverend Mr Brown, who was beginning a wedding service as a fox flashed past the church. With no more ado, he cast off his surplice to reveal riding gear beneath and ran to the rear of the church where his horse was tethered. To a shout of 'Tally Ho!', he vanished and returned to marry the couple next day.

Bobby Dowson's exploits are still discussed in Bilsdale, and the Sun Inn remains in the family which occupied it during his lifetime and long before. The tiny pub even has its own cricket team and private pitch in a nearby steep field.

But there is more history in Bilsdale, because William the Conqueror left his mark in a strange way.

Near Chop Gate is William Beck Farm, close to the head of a stream called William Beck. Its old name was 'Willelmesbec', and this raises the question of the length of folk memory, for Bilsdale has two sayings which link it with the Conqueror. Is this beck also linked to the Conqueror's historic journey along this dale?

Upon completion of his infamous Harrying of the North during the autumn and winter of 1069, William and his army decided to return to York from Teesside. Their most direct route was via Bilsdale, but a severe snowstorm occurred. Somewhere in Bilsdale, William and six of his mounted escort became separated from the main body of his army, and spent all night seeking them. The story goes that William cursed and shouted as he sought them, the sound of his angry foreign language terrifying local people. They remained indoors, fearful that he would attack them, and memories of that awful cursing live on today. From that time, we have two sayings. One is 'cussing like Billy Norman', and the other is 'when Billy the Norman kept hisself warm wi' swearing'.

There is another, more light-hearted tale too. When William was lost and shouting for his men, he came upon a solitary local farmer. In French, he asked the farmer to explain where he was, and also if he had seen anything of the missing army. The farmer did not understand a word and shook his head, whereupon William cursed him and called him '*espèce d'idiot*'. The farmer replied, 'Aye, mebbe so, but Ah'm not lost.'

While it is the River Seph which flows gently down Bilsdale, it is the Rye which meanders past Rievaulx and the dramatic

Terrace with its Temples; the meeting place of the rivers is below the flat-topped hill called Easterside, near Hawnby. There the Seph enters the young Rye which has made its enchanting way from Snilesworth Moor, at times travelling alongside the narrow road from Osmotherley. After moving through thickly wooded glens and ravines, it ripples past Hawnby, a lofty village which clings precariously to a steep moorland hillside. One reference calls it 'a faraway spot', but it was originally a Danish settlement called Halmi's Farm. Now its houses seem to cling together for warmth or companionship, and a flow of spring water gurgles down the village in a specially made gutter.

Below the village, on the banks of the gentle Rye, is the tiny church of All Saints, whose graveyard is a tumble of tombstones. When I called, it was pretty with snowdrops, and the only sounds were the ripple of the river and the call of the rooks. The church lays no claim to any priceless treasures of wood, stone or glass, but it has been here since the twelfth century and there are Norman towers in the south wall. The huge iron hinges on the main door cannot fail to attract the eye, while near the font is a curious stone cross, some two feet high, with a circle engraved on each of its four arms.

Today the little church is served from Old Byland, but Hawnby features as the first stronghold of Methodism in this area. This arose when some men of Hawnby wished to follow that faith but found great opposition. Their problem reached the ears of John Wesley, who came to Hawnby on 7 July 1757 and found his followers had been thrown out of their homes. Some had been prosecuted for disturbing the peace. This visit stirred Wesley's followers into action; they bought their own cottages outside the village and created a flourishing group of Methodists. A chapel was built in 1770 and enlarged in 1814 or 1815. The present chapel is believed to occupy that same site.

Of interest near Hawnby is Arden Hall, a seventeenth-century house deep in a wooded valley to the west of the village, the seat of the earls of Mexborough. Portions of a chimney are believed to date from an ancient nunnery which occupied the site and an old legend said that so long as this chimney shall stand, the owner of Upsall Castle shall pay to the Lord of Arden the sum of £40 per year. Lord Tranmire, the present owner of Upsall Castle, tells me he has no knowledge of the legend, and it does not appear in his grandfather's manuscript history of Upsall.

However, as far back as 1540 there were financial links between Upsall and Arden. The Tancreds of Arden were the 'great money-lenders of Yorkshire', and Robert Rosse of Upsall became involved in 'inextricable monetary difficulties'. When Dr John Turton bought Upsall Estate in 1778, there was a rent charge of £40 per annum payable to the Tancreds of Arden, but it seems that Lord Tranmire's grandfather or uncle may have bought out this charge.

There is a Nun's Well in the grounds too, and Mary, Queen of Scots, reputedly spent a night here.

To the east of Bilsdale's broad valley lies the central bulk of the Moors. The high land sends its crystal waters north into Eskdale and south into the Rye, and it is those other southern-bound dales that we now examine.

To the south of that central ridge, the topography is different from that of Eskdale. For one thing, the landscape is less rugged and bleak, and the houses are of a different style. While those to the north of the Moors are of dark granite with blue slate roofs, many of those in the south are of pale yellow sandstone with red pantiles and brick chimneystacks. The southern valleys are broader and more fertile, with rich arable crops and gentle deciduous woodland. But even so, those dales which cast their waters into the Rye have their heads deep in the rugged Moors, almost meeting with the heads of the northern dales. Bransdale and Farndale almost meet near Cockayne Ridge just south of Baysdale Moor, while Rosedale lies south of Danby, Fryup and Glaisdale.

Lovely Newton Dale, with its nostalgic steam railway, runs like a ravine towards the valley of the Murk Esk, while the conifer-lined dales of Allerston Forest discharge their waters into the River Derwent. This flows serenely through Forge Valley, and the Rye and other rivers from the moors meet the Derwent south of Pickering.

The two parts of the Moors, the north represented by Eskdale and the south by Ryedale, rarely communicated in bygone times. There were few tracks across the hills, the main one perhaps being the road through Rosedale which divided, and indeed still divides, to carry one route over the moors to Castleton and the other into the Eskdale via Glaisdale or Egton Bridge.

Between Rosedale and Glaisdale, some 1,065 feet above sea-level, was the lonely but vital Hamer Inn, known in 1858 as the Lettered Board. It was a place of refreshment and refuge for those who made that perilous trip between the dales, but it fell into disuse in the 1930s. I can recall the chill moorland winds sighing around the sturdy walls of the old inn, but now only an insignificant heap of stones and a patch of uncharacteristic green grass remain. The well which supplied the occupants and travellers with fresh water was recently filled in and covered to prevent accidents. The site continues as a place of refreshment, if only for tourists having picnics there, and hikers on the Lyke Wake Walk pausing during their trek.

Coal was mined nearby as recently as 1926, when the General Strike brought it to an end, and it was the favourite stopping place within the last hundred years for carriers who brought loads of limestone from Ryedale into Eskdale.

From Hamer, where two travellers mysteriously died one night, it is possible to look across the Moors to Fylingdales Early Warning Station and into the spread of the tree-lined southern dales.

One of them is Rosedale, a bewitching place whose name is not derived from the flower. It comes instead from the Old Norse personal name of Russi and means Russi's Valley. Of Rosedale, Murray's Handbook for Travellers in Yorkshire, published in 1874 says, 'The charm of these dales is only half discovered by those who merely pass up and down them. They should come upon them suddenly, from the dreary heathland which protects and isolates them, with which they are in admirable contrast.' I agree entirely, for one of the finest views in this part of the Moors is from the top of Rosedale's steep Chimney Bank. This hill, with gradients that must be approaching one in two (about forty-five per cent) in places (if that is possible), is now open to light vehicular traffic, but the summit offers a magnificent, almost aerial view of the broad dale below.

The name comes from a huge hundred-foot-high brick chimney which once occupied this site. It was a relic of Rosedale's Klondike-style iron-ore boom of the last century and a landmark for miles around. Sadly, in 1972 it was declared dangerous and therefore felled, so removing one of the best-known landmarks of the Moors.

Nearby, and in the dale below, are further reminders of that hectic period, although Rosedale, like so many of the other moorland dales, had witnessed iron-ore mining centuries earlier. Iron Age man probably worked iron here, and the monks of Byland Abbey came to mine their ore. Rosedale had forges in 1209, and in 1328 Edward II granted some nuns land for iron-ore working. But none of this was on the scale of the nineteenth-century boom. At first, Rosedale's iron was rejected because of its inferior quality, but subsequent discoveries showed that it was excellent, and furthermore, huge quantities awaited those who could extract it.

The first mine was opened in 1851 by George Leeman of York, an MP and railway magnate, and it yielded more than three million tons of ore between 1856 and 1885. Others followed and soon Rosedale's peaceful, rural landscape was transformed into a bustling, noisy industrial valley with chapels, miners' cottages, a hospital, engine sheds, warehouses, coal depots, workshops and shops, with an amazing railway line constructed around the rim of the dale. One wonders whether this spectacular route was among the first to cater for sightseers. Essentially a mining line, it struggled up the dale and over the Moors to Ingleby Greenhow, where it linked with the then North Yorkshire and Cleveland line. Its journey provided such outstanding views that the proprietors of the mine in Rosedale allowed passengers to be carried along the picturesque track. Its route is still visible.

In 1851 the population of Rosedale was around 550; by 1874 an additional six hundred men were employed, and at its peak the little village hosted some five thousand workers and found itself having to cope with such unaccustomed problems as lack of entertainment, disturbances through drunkenness and fights over women. There was damage too. The workers raided Rosedale's ancient ruined abbey and used the stones to build a lecture hall and a schoolroom. This incredible boom continued for seventy years, but by the 1920s, it was declining, and the end followed the General Strike in 1926. The last train ran along the Rosedale railway line in 1928.

Gradually the dale returned to normal. Today it still bears signs of those dramatic times, and their impact lingers in the minds of the older people. My own grandfather worked there for a time and walked the twenty or so miles from Skinningrove across the Moors to obtain employment. Today, though, Rosedale is at peace, and its only influx is a seasonal one of tourists.

Rosedale's near neighbour is Farndale, a valley noted among other things for its ancient cruck houses and thatched cottages, several of which survived into the 1970s. One or two remain and, indeed, thatching continues to be a living skill in Ryedale, where numbers of thatched cottages are occupied. The Star Inn, some distance away at Harome near Helmsley, is a charming example. With its white walls and clematis sprawling across the thatch, it makes a pleasing picture.

Farndale's name may come from the Gaelic *fearna*, which indicates links with the alder, a flourishing tree of the riverside, or it might come from fern, but it is noted for another pretty plant – the daffodil. Millions of small wild yellow daffodils grow along both banks of the pleasing River Dove and extend six or seven miles along the dale. There are other flowers, but none compares with the sheer volume of daffodils. Several varieties grow, but the reason for this phenomenon is not known. No one can be sure why they arrived or why they are so numerous; one legend attributes them to the monks of Rievaulx who planted them during their travels, and another claim is that they were introduced to Farndale by Nicholas Postgate, the Egton Bridge martyr. They do grow around his home village too, and in Glaisdale Dale, and he called them 'Lenten Lilies', a name commonly used in some areas of the Moors.

It is curious, however, that topographical books published before the turn of the century omit references to the daffodils of Farndale, and it was the advent of the motor car which introduced them to a wider audience. Maybe they are a modern innovation to the dale? Once the news of their presence reached the outer world, greedy visitors came in their thousands to plunder the flowers; many plants were trampled underfoot, and some people even brought scythes and sickles to mow them! Car boots were filled by traders who sold them on the markets, and the bulbs were uprooted for re-planting in urban gardens. In a very short time, the daffodils were at risk of being obliterated, and just over thirty years ago this greed became a very real threat. In 1953 the North Riding County Council declared two thousand acres of the dale a local Nature Reserve, with a byelaw forbidding the unauthorized picking of the flower or lifting of the bulbs.

When I was a policeman in the area, one of my annual duties, along with many of my colleagues, was to patrol Farndale, partly with an eye on the daffodils but chiefly to enforce a one-way traffic system around the dale. This Daffodil Route became necessary to ensure a free flow of traffic around narrow, steep roads of the valley. But little can be seen from a moving vehicle. The only way is to park in one of the official car-parks and follow the footpaths among the flowers as they bloom in April.

The daffodil season is a short one, and my advice would be to visit them either during the early morning or in the evening when other visitors are not there. I was pleased to see some distinguished visitors adopting this advice, for one early morning I arrived in full police motor-cycling gear and was greeted by Their Royal Highnesses the Duke and Duchess of Kent, as they ended an early morning stroll among the flowers.

Another threat came in the late 1960s when the upper dale was selected by Hull Corporation as a possible site for a reservoir. It would fill a natural basin above Church Houses and so provide water for Humberside, but the plan was never approved. And so the daffodils of Farndale survive to please us during the spring. I often wonder if they were here when Wordsworth visited the North Riding of Yorkshire.

Farndale's remoteness has given rise to several legends and tales of hobs which are related in Chapter 9.

Across the hills lies Bransdale, an isolated community of a few scattered farms without the benefit of a village. Until 1935 the dale boasted Bransdale Mill, probably the only oatmeal mill in the Moors. At its head is Bransdale Lodge, used as a shooting lodge by the Earls of Feversham, and nearby is a church dedicated to Saints Nicholas and Mary, re-built in 1886 after the previous building fell into disuse after the Reformation. There is another church in Bransdale too, the tiny, lonely church of St Mary Magdalen not far from the foot of Cowhouse Bank, surrounded by pine woods and huge nests of wood ants.

Today Bransdale is purely agricultural, much of it owned by the National Trust, although in the past it has seen the mining of iron ore, jet and coal and some limestone quarrying.

Until the 1950s the dale was almost inaccessible, then radio telephones helped to ease the problems of communication, but even now farmers facing one another across the dale must undergo a long, narrow, winding route if they wish to visit one another or seek mutual aid. The narrow, gated road still meanders up one side of the dale from Helmsley and emerges later in Kirkbymoorside, having traversed well over twenty noteworthy miles. When I took my daughter around the dale for a driving lesson, the road was thick with tiny wild rabbits and wandering sheep, with birds and flowers all around in the high hedgerows. There is solitude and rural peace up there.

Bransdale's river is Hodge Beck, which flows into Sleightholmedale where there was once a spa with lilies in Lily Wood, and then into Kirkdale where it passed the ancient Minster and Cave. Near Kirkdale, it disappears underground, seeping through its stony bed into the limestone beneath to emerge some distance downstream. This disappearing trick lends support to the notion that underground hereabouts is a vast complex of limestone caves and even a reservoir. There is such a reservoir not far away, at Ness, which serves the domestic requirements of the district. Heavy rain can increase the water's flow until it is a full river, washing across the ford near Kirkdale Minster and joining the River Dove south of Welburn.

The rivers from all these dales take us to the southern edge of the Moors, where, close to Pickering, is Thornton le Dale, one of several villages said to be Yorkshire's prettiest, but in 1907 this *was* voted the prettiest village in Yorkshire! The National Park boundary loops so as to contain this gem, whose name comes from 'Thorn Ton', 'a village enclosed by a thorn hedge'. Its older name is Thornton le Dale but modern usage has shortened this by omitting the 'le'.

Bubbling streams flow among the houses, and one runs beside the main road, once separated from it only by a white line. On very wet days, drivers would confuse the river with the road, and many have been startled to find themselves up to the hubcaps in Thornton Beck. Now a raised footpath provides a useful boundary. Few villages of such charm have a main road running through the centre.

Tiny bridges and gardens full of flowers adorn the stream which flows from the depths of Dalby Forest, and at the point, where it enters the village beneath the A170, can be seen Beck

Isle Cottage, one of the most photographed of England's thatched cottages. So beautifully proportioned and well maintained is this house beside the stream that it finds itself in calendars, chocolate boxes and magazine covers and in advertisements of all kinds. When I called in the summer of 1984, its frontage was ablaze with colour; a multitude of brilliant blooms made this exquisite sight a genuine and unforgettable picture.

Almost opposite is the Hall, a fine Tudor building now an hotel with an extensive car-park in its grounds. Access is from the road to Malton.

One little known aspect of Thornton le Dale is its castle. It used to exist about a mile along the road towards Pickering, but the only evidence now consists of some unimposing green mounds. It was known as Roxby Castle, home of the Cholmleys. Sir Richard Cholmley, in the time of Elizabeth I, was known as 'The Great Black Knight of the North', and he was noted for his hospitality at the castle. He died there in 1578 and is buried in the parish church of All Saints, which dates from around 1200. The graveyard contains the body of Matthew Grimes, who died in 1875, aged ninety-six. An old soldier, he stood guard over Napoleon at St Helena and helped carry him to his grave.

Other features of Thornton le Dale include a six-hundred-year-old market cross and a set of stocks on the tiny green at the crossroads, plus Lady Lumley's twelve almshouses at the side of the A170. These were completed in 1670 and are still in use, but the old grammar school, which she founded in 1657 and which stands at the end of them, ceased to be a grammar school in 1899. John Wesley is said to have preached at Box Tree Farm, and there is a busy animal-feed mill tucked discreetly into a corner of the village. The shops, inns, cafés and forge are all reasons for savouring this lovely place and off the main thoroughfares are many interesting sights and walks. There is enough to fill a whole day, and nearby Ellerburn is worth a call.

The villages between here and Scarborough are not within the National Park's boundaries; neither do they claim to be moorland villages. Nonetheless, they are worthy of mention because of their proximity to the Moors. They sit beautifully in a broad valley rich with growing crops and leafy woodlands; their charms tend to be ignored by passing drivers, for each straddles

Staithes at low tide with Boulby Cliff

Women wearing the traditional Staithes bonnet, *c.* 1965

Sandsend *c.* 1960 showing the railway viaduct before its demolition

The 1957 Horngarth Ceremony – planting the Penny Hedge at Whitby

Whitby at night from the new bridge

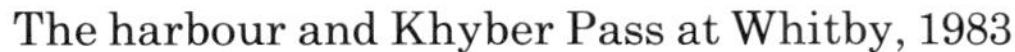

The harbour and Khyber Pass at Whitby, 1983

A woodland path near Grosmont

Opposite: Beggar's Bridge, Glaisdale

Thomas Watson's photograph of Eskdale following the disastrous floods of 1930. This railway bridge lay between Glaisdale and Egton Bridge and has since been replaced by a modern structure

Shandy Hall, Coxwold, once the home of Laurence Sterne

Rosedale, once a thriving ironstone mining community, is now a peaceful and beautiful valley

The Star Inn at Harome and (*below*) the restored Sun Inn at Bilsdale

Farndale with Blakey Ridge in the background

Ravenscar towards Robin Hood's Bay showing stooks of corn

the A170 which carries busy coast-bound traffic, and yet there are some interesting aspects to them.

Probably the only item of interest in Wilton, however, is the re-built church with its Norman font and medieval pillars, but Allerston and Ebberston between them have provided us with an historical puzzle dating from the Commonwealth period, when Charles II was in exile. It comes from depositions heard at York Assizes from which it seems that, about two weeks before Christmas 1656, a Robert Awderson was out riding a grey gelding when he met a man called Matthew Vasey, who lived at Marishes, near Pickering. Vasey began to admire Awderson's horse and surprised Awderson by saying that if he would give the animal to King Charles, he would be paid £500 in due course. Vasey went on to say that three men, one of whom was Charles II, had passed through Ebberston and had gone to a house in Allerston 'to lye downe on a bedde there and gett some potchett [poached eggs] and before day northwards went upon horses, each of about ten pounds price'.

Whether this was a skilful confidence trick or whether Charles II (1660–85) did sleep and eat poached eggs at Allerston may never be known. What is known is that the Cayley family of nearby Brompton had been closely linked to the sovereign since the time of Edward I, and their devotion to the Stuarts produced a knighthood in 1641, and a baronetcy in 1661. Charles came to the throne in 1660 and Sir William Cayley was mayor of Scarborough in 1686, being mentioned in a charter of incorporation given to the town by Charles II. So Charles did have friends in the area, and maybe he did come here in disguise?

Allerston's tiny, aisleless church is interesting enough to justify a call, while at Ebberston a curious event is commemorated by a field called Bloody Field. It is claimed that King Aldfrith of Northumbria (685–704) fought his father here. Aldfrith's name is spelt variously as Alhfrith, Alcfrith, or Alfrid (the latter being pronounced Alfred), and his father was Oswy, who reigned from 642 to 670, first as King of Bernicia and then as King of all Northumbria.

It seems there was constant friction between father and son because Aldfrith attended the Synod of Whitby and argued against his father. But the Battle of Ebberston was, according to legend, more vicious, because Aldfrith was stabbed and died among some rocks. Some say he was merely injured and rested there before travelling to Driffield where he died. The opening where he fell was called King Alfred's Cave. However, Bede's account of this king says he died naturally at Driffield on 14 December 704.

So there is a mystery, although Bede's account gives the location of this incident as Scamridge Dykes. These are remarkable early earthworks which occupy some three square miles of moorland above Allerston and Ebberston. They are a series of mounds and ditches probably dating from the Stone Age and high enough in places to shield a mounted man. Fourteen bodies dating a thousand years BC were found here in the last century, and a communal dwelling with a thatched roof was also discovered. It seems a likely place for a battle between a warring father and son. Indeed, in 1790 Sir Charles Hotham erected a shelter here to commemorate that fight.

The road from Snainton through delightful Troutsdale passes across some earthworks. Pause awhile at the car-park near the beech trees, to savour the atmosphere and the serene views. There are bilberries here too.

The Cockmoor Hall Forest Drive begins nearby and takes a memorable route into Dalby Forest.

Back upon the main road from Ebberston lies Snainton, a pretty collection of houses among which is a lovely Norman archway, renovated since its foundation and forming a lych-gate leading to the parish church. This arch belonged to an earlier church, although the present one does contain a Norman font which was once used as a farm trough!

It was at Snainton in the seventeenth century that Robert Hendley attempted to create a type of Gretna Green by marrying people outside the church. Because he had no authority to conduct such weddings, he was charged that, between 1649 and 1650, he had married couples without the consent of their parents, 'nor doth he in any publicke manner make known the intencion of theire marriage according to the lawes of the land, but in private plaus and at unlawful houres doeth make itt his practice to joyne any men and women together in wedlocke not of his parish'.

Nearby is Brompton, one of several North Yorkshire villages of this name; this one tends to sit reticently alongside the A170, although it has a good deal to boast about. It used to be the residence of the kings of Northumbria who played such a vital part in the early history of the Moors: their residence was sited on Castle Hill. Brompton is also said to have been the birthplace of John de Brompton, a monk of Whitby who later became abbot of Jervaulx Abbey. He was noted for his chronicle of events from the arrival of St Augustine to the time of Richard I.

There was a church here at the time of the Domesday survey, and Brompton's present church, which dates to around the fourteenth century, is of interest because it was here on 4 October 1802 that William Wordsworth married local girl Mary Hutchinson. She lived at Gallows Hill Farm on the road to Scarborough.

But Brompton's unsung place in history comes from the work of the local squire, Sir George Cayley, an inventive genius and without doubt a great pioneer of flying. As early as 1804 – ninety-nine years before the Wright brothers' first sustained power flight – Sir George experimented with a type of glider. He realized that the flapping wings of a bird were useless for manned flights and constructed a kite upon a pole which even had a moveable cross-shaped tail. He flew this down a hillside and said, 'It was very pretty to see it sail down a steep hill.' He noted that the rudder movements caused it to change direction, but at this stage his glider did not carry a man. None the less, he envisaged a man travelling on such a device, believing it would be safer than a mule for descending the Alps, and by 1809 had produced a glider large enough to lift off the ground anyone who tried to hold onto it in flight.

This 1809 flight is said to be the first known flight by a full-size scientifically designed aircraft, and Cayley had even used a whirling arm or propeller to help the flight. But these early aircraft were gliders, for they lacked engines.

He next produced a tension wheel for his gliders to land upon, and from this idea was developed the spoked wheel of the pedal cycle. By 1849 he had developed a machine with fixed wings, adjustable controls and a light three-wheeled undercarriage. On this, a boy of ten was floated off the ground for several yards down a hill, but one wonders whether he did anything to control the flight.

Then, in 1853, came Cayley's triumph. With one of his machines Sir George and his entourage went into nearby

Brompton Dale and selected a man to sit upon it. This was Sir George's coachman. Aboard this early aircraft, he flew from the high east side of the valley across to the west, a distance of about fifty yards. But when he landed, the coachman shouted, 'Sir George, I wish to give notice. I was hired to drive, not to fly.'

Fifty-one years later, the Wright brothers fitted an engine to a machine of similar design, something envisaged by Sir George, and flew it at Kitty Hawk in North Carolina.

It was the same Sir George Cayley who suggested the impressive Sea Cut mentioned on page 74 and so prevented the River Derwent flooding around Malton and Pickering.

He was truly a Yorkshireman of genius and died at Brompton Hall in 1857. A hang-gliding club which flies on the North York Moors at the Hole of Horcum is named after him – the George Cayley Sailwing Club.

At Wykeham, the National Park boundary returns to the A170, where it goes on to slice through West and East Ayton before veering over Irton Moor, then skirts around to Scalby to join the coast near Hundale Point.

At Wykeham there is a curious lych-gate outside the parish church. It is noteworthy because it is in fact the tower of an earlier church and stands away from the main building. For this reason, it has given birth to a legend which says that two sisters decided to build a church but quarrelled before it was completed. One therefore built the tower and the other the main body of the church, each a respectful distance from the other. This type of yarn is linked to other churches in England and in this case has no foundation.

It is known that there was a Cistercian nunnery at Wykeham in 1153, but it was far from wealthy and the priory was destroyed by fire in the reign of Edward III. In the fourteenth century a chapel was founded here by John de Wykeham and dedicated to St Mary and St Helen, but in time this fell into disrepair. The surviving tower was restored, and a cross marks the site of the old altar, but the old chapel was demolished to make way for the present church, completed in 1853, after being designed by William Butterfield. He had made a special study of medieval Gothic architecture and worked on many parish churches. It was Butterfield who put the finishing touches to the tower at Wykeham, making it a unique lych-gate, but the interior of the church is also worth a visit. It contains exquisite oak carved by the Kilburn craftsman Mousey Thompson.

The modern Wykeham Abbey, where bananas once grew, is now the seat of Viscount Downe.

The twin villages of Ayton are divided by a handsome stone bridge which spans the Derwent, and the road along the picturesque Forge Valley, a National Nature Reserve, emerges here, as does another leading into the wooded Yedmandale. These villages have developed into dormitory areas for nearby Scarborough and are blessed with beautiful surrounding countryside. The Moors around Silpho and Broxa are outstanding and provide ranging views across the hills and coast, but it is the spa town of Scarborough which dominates this south-east corner of the Moors.

Now, by way of complete contrast, I will sweep diagonally across the inland Moors and head north-west into one of our least-known dales. It is set apart from all the others because its waters flow into neither the Esk nor the Rye, although its gentle green pastures do push into the moors at the edge of the Cleveland Hills. This is Scugdale, whose tiny beck crosses a ford and enters Swainby almost secretly before winding its way north into the River Leven and then into the Tees.

But first we'll look at some nearby villages. Swainby has all the appearances of a modern village but in fact dates to the fourteenth century, when the people of Whorlton moved from their hilltop site and settled here. Much of its ancient history was lost when, about a century ago, it became the mecca of miners seeking ironstone, many of whom came to spend their earnings. They used donkeys for carrying coal and their domestic goods, and grazed them on Live Moor. Their influence lives on in the name of the Miners' Arms public house, and some cottages still known as the Miners' Cottages. While compiling this book, I found one of them which had been put on the market. It had no hot water, no inside toilet and no modern refinements. It was practically unchanged from its appearance a century ago, when it was occupied by a miner and his family.

In the shadow of Carlton Bank, known for its gliding club, ancient alum quarries and modern motorcycle scrambling course, stands the charming Carlton-in-Cleveland with its Alum Beck, just within the Park. Alum shale is unique to the North

York Moors and between 1600 and 1880 was extensively mined for use in the tanning and cloth industries. There were more than twenty alum quarries on the Moors. Its church bears witness to the work of a dedicated parson. When George Sangar arrived in the last century to find a derelict church, he set about building a new one. He worked day and night both on the building and raising cash and did all his own labouring. He even carried the stones as he built a church of which the village was proud. He finished it in 1881 but soon afterwards fire broke out and destroyed everything he had done. He was then charged with setting fire to his own church, but was acquitted. Another church, St Botolph's, now occupies the site, with its tower half in and half out of the nave. This was started in 1896, and a lych-gate followed in 1912.

Carlton-in-Cleveland was the home of the legendary farming parson Canon J.L.Kyle, who bred black-faced moorland sheep, ran three farms, owned the village pub, rode with the hunt and at the same time ministered to his moorland parish in a unique way. He died in 1943 after being vicar for almost fifty years, and descendants of his family (and his flock of sheep!) are still in the district.

There is one story which sums up his earthy attitude. A farmer whose crops were dying came to ask Canon Kyle to pray for rain. In the language of the farmer, the worthy Canon replied, 'Thoo doesn't want rain, thoo wants muck.'

Nearby is quiet Faceby, where a mole unearthed a Roman bracelet and left it on its mound for a ploughman to find and where, on Whorl Hill, a hoard of silver bars was unearthed. These might have been plundered from nearby Whorlton Castle. At Faceby, until very recently, a curious dole was issued each week to twelve poor people. Twelve charity loaves worth a penny each were given to them in accordance with the will of Anthony Lazenby, a merchant tailor of London who died on 20 September 1634. The will stipulated that the dole be issued for all time, the money for it being collected from four farms in the area. When buying these properties, the owners also acquired the duty of paying their share of the dole, and the money was collected by the vicar. By 1960 the money was given to the village shopkeeper, who issued it to deserving people. When I spoke to Mrs Alice Bensley, the shopkeeper, she told me that until 1982 she received the collected monies and from them gave four people a 10p loaf each Saturday. Since then, it seems, the dole has not been collected or distributed. There is no vicar at Faceby now, and the State cares for the poor. It is 350 years since Anthony Lazenby said the dole should continue 'for all time'. His wishes have fallen prey to progress.

But one custom does continue at Faceby, and indeed at other churches in the area. After a wedding, the groom and best man stand at the church gate and throw pennies to the children. A similar event still occurs on St Swithin's Day (15 July), when the Lord of the Manor of Seamer, near Scarborough, tosses newly minted coins to infant-school children.

Near Faceby is secluded and charming Scugdale, (probably a lake in prehistoric times), less than three miles long, with a hamlet called Huthwaite about half way. In the 1800s there was some ironstone mining here, but no trace remains. But it has produced two remarkable people. One was called Henry Cooper, and the other was Elizabeth Harland. Elizabeth died in 1812, having achieved fame by living until she was 105, while Henry was a giant who in 1890 had grown to a height of eight feet six inches. He was then the world's tallest living man and, after working as a farm labourer, joined Barnum and Bailey's Circus, to tour America with them and the famous Jumbo the Elephant. Cooper married a tall woman from the circus, but died in England at thirty-two years of age.

9

Tales to be told

Should you ask me whence these stories,
Whence these legends and traditions?
Henry Wadsworth Longfellow (1807–82)

As a schoolboy, one of my pleasures was to visit my friend at Hart Hall Farm, Glaisdale, where we would sit and chat by the flickering kitchen fire in its old-fashioned iron range. Crickets chirped in the shadows of the fireside; the lighting was by oil lamps, and on a dark autumn night the winds howled about the chimneys as snug cattle fidgeted in the lonely outbuildings. In some ways it was like stepping back a century or more, for this farm is the reputed haunt of one of North Yorkshire's many hobs.

Hobs and goblins feature in the folklore of many countries, but the hobs of the North York Moors are usually depicted as very solitary, dwarf-like creatures who live with a particular family and perform odd jobs around the farm. They are often shaggy-haired and ugly, and many work naked and detest clothes to the extent of regarding a gift of clothing as an insult. Such a gift tends to annoy them intensely, upon which they become mischievous or even vindictive and dangerous. Hobs are adept at hiding themselves from prying eyes; they work extremely hard and very quickly but seek no reward except an occasional word of thanks.

This is a very general outline, and details of them and their behaviour do vary from place to place. Examples of other hob-goblins include the Cauld Lad of Hilton Castle in Northumberland, the *bwca* of Monmouthshire, the Danish *nisse*, the redcaps of Holland and Scotland, the *tomtars* of Sweden, the leprechauns of Ireland, the buggane of the Isle of Man, along with Puck, pixies, banshees, brownies, imps and many others.

But in the North York Moors we call them hobs. Evidence of their role in our folklore remains in the names of locations like Hob Cross, Hob Hill, Hob Green, Hob Thrush Grange, Hob Dale, Hob's Cave, Hob Holes and Hob Garth. Furthermore, some very impressive stories remain in North Riding folklore, and among them is the tale of the Hart Hall Hob. It has a ring of authenticity about it.

The Hob of Glaisdale's Hart Hall was a kindly fellow who performed good deeds and was loved by the occupants of the farm. He preferred to work about the midnight hours, always in secret.

One illustrative yarn tells of his help when a hay wagon wheel became wedged between two stones. Bad weather was threatening, and it was vital that the hay was brought in from the fields without delay. But this wheel was stuck fast; extra horses and men were drafted in to release it but all the efforts failed. The only solution was to unload the hay, a time-consuming task, but night came all too quickly and it was decided to leave the load *in situ* overnight; it would have to be tackled first thing next morning. As the tired workers fell into bed, the hob got to work. With his superior strength, he released the wheel with the wagon fully loaded, then drew it into the yard, unloaded it and stacked the hay. He even prepared the wagon for the following day's work.

This was just one of many good deeds. He was always available when required, and there was never any need to ask. He assisted with the threshing, ploughing, sowing, harrowing, stacking and general work on the farm. But this was always done in secret; no one ever saw him at work or even heard him.

Except once. And here we have an account, in dialect, from an elderly lady. It seems it was a moonlit night in the autumn when a worker happened to hear a flail threshing inside a closed barn. The hob was at work. At last there was an opportunity to see him.

This is how she told the story. 'Yah moonleeght neeght, when they heeard his swipple gannan wiv a strange quick bat o' t'lathe fleear (ye ken he wad deea mair i' yah neeght than a' t'men o' t'farm iv a deea), yan o' t'lads gat hissel croppen oop close anenst lathe-deear, an' leeaked in thruff a lahtle hole i' t'boards, an' he seen a lahtle brown man, a' covered wi' hair, spangin' aboot wiv t'fleeal lahk yan wad.

'He'd getten a haill dess o' shaffs doon on t'fleear and My Wod! Ommost afore ye could tell ten, he had tonned out t'strae, an' sided away t'coorn, and was rife for another dess. He had neea clothes on ti speeak of and t'lad, he could see 'at he had neea mak or mander o' duds bar an aud ragged soort o' sark.'

Because it appeared that the little man had nothing but a ragged shirt to wear (the sark), and as the autumn nights were growing colder, the staff of Hart Hall, upon hearing this tale, decided to make a suit for the little fellow. They decided to 'mak him summat ti hap hisself wiv', and they produced a rough working shirt made from hessian, with a belt around the middle. It never occurred to them that it might be offensive to the hob, or that he might object to their having spied on him at work. When it was finished, they took it to the barn and laid it ready for his next visit. Once more, they secretly watched as he picked it up, turned it over and examined it. He then realized he was being watched, but it seems he was surprisingly sweet-tempered because he turned to his benefactors and explained that hobs must work almost naked. In his own words, this is how he explained it:

Gin hob mun hae nowt but a hardin hamp,
He'll cum nae mair, nowther to berry nor stamp.

And then he left Hart Hall.

Another favourite story concerns the Farndale Hob. He lived with a farmer called Jonathan Gray who was hard-working and very businesslike. This hob aided him in his work, having apparently attached himself to the farm when Jonathan's grandfather worked it. He had come to the aid of the old man after a worker died in a ferocious snowstorm, and some felt the hob was the spirit of that worker. He worked hard all the time, thrashing, carting hay, mowing, shearing sheep and doing all manner of essential tasks. In this way he helped Jonathan's grandfather and father, his only reward being a nightly jug of cream left in the barn. Year in and year out, he worked for the Grays, and when Jonathan and his young wife took over, the same system continued. Jonathan prospered and the farm was one of the most efficient in Farndale. Although Jonathan's wife died, the work continued until he re-married.

Then disaster struck. Unfortunately, Jonathan's new wife was mean with money and complained that it was wasteful to leave a jug of cream in the barn for something or someone she had never seen. One night she left a jug of skimmed milk instead of cream, and at that stage the hob stopped his work. Instead he became mischievous, and for poor Jonathan things started to go wrong. Foxes attacked his geese and hens, the cheese always turned sour, the house became haunted by a poltergeist which terrified the servants, and in no time at all the situation was appalling. Jonathan was reduced from a successful, wealthy farmer to a nervous wreck with a severely ailing business. The only solution was to move and start anew.

He and his wife found a nice farm a few miles away and loaded their few remaining belongings onto a cart. With his wife at his side, Jonathan began his journey, but only a short distance down the dale they met a neighbour, who called, 'Noo then, Jonathan, what's gahin' on?'

'We're flitting,' said Jonathan sadly.

And to his horror, the lid of a milk churn on his cart was raised and a little wizened brown face peered out. 'Aye,' said the hob. 'We're flitting.'

So the unfortunate Jonathan had no choice – he turned around and went back to his old farm and to all his old problems.

Links with Farndale Hob remain in a rocky outcrop called Obtrusch, or Hob Thrush.

These, and the Runswick Bay Hob mentioned in Chapter 6, are perhaps the best known of the moorland hobs, but others did exist around and within the North York Moors. Hobs lived in caves near Mulgrave Castle, and in cliffs on the edge of the Hambleton Hills near Sutton Bank. It was here that Hob Thrush Hall existed – a cave which contained a supernatural creature, and the road from the North Riding into Durham was haunted by a hob known as Hob Headless. He was unable to cross the river between the two counties and terrified all who used that stretch of road. Legend says that he was exorcized and lies buried beneath a large rock beside that road. He will remain there for ninety-nine years and a day, and anyone unfortunate enough to sit on that rock will be unable to leave it. It lies somewhere between Hurworth and Neasham near Darlington – indeed, another hob lived at Coniscliffe, and Durham had others at Hartlepool and Sunderland.

Castleton in Eskdale had a hob too, and others recorded on the Moors include the Cross Hob of Lastingham, Elphi of Low Farndale, Hodge Hob of Bransdale, Hob of Hasty Bank in Bilsdale, Dale Town Hob of Hawnby, Hob of Chop Gate, the Goathland Hob of Howl Moor, Hob of Egton High Moor and the Scugdale Hob.

There may be others whose legendary exploits have faded with the passage of time but the ones named above are those which survived in our moorland folklore.

But if tales of hobs continue to feature in moorland folk memory, so do tales of witch-hares and witches. The belief in witch-hares was not solely British for it was widely believed across Europe that witches could turn themselves into animal forms such as frogs and cats.

The most persistent stories within the North York Moors were that some local witches could turn themselves into hares. This lingered within living memory, and practically all the stories have the same foundations. A hare is put up by the hounds and flees towards the house of a known or suspected witch. It manages to get inside to safety, and when the hunters enter, they find it has adopted the form of the suspected witch, who bears all the signs of having been hunted. Sometimes the hounds manage to nip the leg of the fleeing hare, or a hunter manages to hit it with a shot; in these cases, the witch is found to have a corresponding injury to her body, but she usually provides a convincing explanation for her condition. Death rarely comes because a witch-hare could be killed only with a silver bullet.

One tale which has undoubtedly been exaggerated through re-telling concerns Peg Humphrey of East Moors above Helmsley. It was told to Major J. Fairfax-Blakeborough by Bobby Dowson, the Bilsdale Huntsman (see page 151) who would be around twenty years old at the time of this incident, and it confirms that the belief existed well into the last century.

Bobby and some colleagues were hunting hares and put up one which made straight for Peg's home, where it vanished through a hole in the barn door. The lads followed and opened the barn door to find Peg lying on the straw, panting heavily. 'I've been foddering,' she gasped. 'The barn door blew shut.' On another occasion, Bobby Dowson chased a hare towards Peg's home, and the hounds managed to nip a leg, tearing off a lump of flesh and fur. It continued its dash for freedom and ran 'straight through Peg's house end'. When the hunters entered the house, Peg was lying on a bed, injured and exhausted, and was treated by a doctor in Helmsley for her injuries. She was lame until she died.

These tales follow the classic pattern of witch-hare stories, and I have a letter from Major J. Fairfax-Blakeborough, who died in 1976 aged ninety-three, in which he gives an account of them as told to him by Bobby Dowson in person. Bobby died in 1902, aged eighty-six.

But I also have an account from the late Bill Agar Weatherill, the grandson of a personal friend of Peg Humphrey. These are his own words:

'Father often told me of things he remembered when a boy at "Spout House", Bilsdale. Living next door to the old "Sun Inn", he saw much coming and going, and one story which I found very interesting was that when he was about ten years old he went with some dealers to drive geese back to Spout House from East Moors; they were buying up geese for Christmas market at Middlesbrough. Now these geese had to walk all the way and they wouldn't want hurrying either; they would have to rest and feed, so where else but in "goose garth". On this particular occasion Peg Humphrey specifically asked the dealers not to take her brood goose, my Father said that they *did*, for he was there and he heard her tell them; he drove the flock away over to Spout House, and Peg's brood goose was amongst them. Father said, "Poor simple old woman, if she'd been as clever as some people said, would she have let them take her brood goose?"

'Peg Humphrey was reputed by some to be a witch, but she was a personal friend of my Grandmother and she was no witch. When she came over into the dale, she would call and have a drink o' tea with my Granny.'

This event occurred in 1860, and while it shows that Peg Humphrey was nothing more than an ordinary countrywoman, it does suggest that folk memories of witches continued on the Moors.

Suspect though it may be, the Peg Humphrey witch-hare story is not the only one to be recounted within the Moors. At

Glaisdale 'no mere ordinary hare' was biting the tops off some young saplings near the dale head, and the angry farmer decided to lay in wait and shoot it. Appreciating that this might be a witch-hare, he loaded his gun with shot made from silver buttons, concealed himself close to his nursery of trees and waited. At the witching hour of midnight, the hare appeared and he described it as 'a greeat foul awd ram-cat of a heear' and said it 'began knepping here and knepping there'. Once again, we have an account of the shooting in lovely dialect. He said, 'It wur stoodying how best ti deea t'maist ill in t'lahtlest tahm. Sae t'chap at wur watching, well, he up wiv his gun and aiming steady, he lat dhrive. My wod, but there was a flaysome shrike! At that, t'heear, sair hot, gat hersel' a sooart o' croppen oot o' t'nossery and hoppled away as wheel as she could an' gat heeam at Aud Maggie's house-end, in a bit o'scroggs at grows on t'bank there.' Aud Maggie was the reputed witch, and when the rough land near her house was searched, nothing was found. The following day, however, she was discovered in bed with some injuries and explained them by saying she had fallen onto some broken glass.

Other similar tales involve the Guisborough witch Jane Grear, who was bitten by a dog when galloping in the shape of a hare, and Peggy Flaunders of Marske-by-Sea, who was hunted as a hare and bitten in the haunch. She died in 1835. Jane Wood was a witch-hare who lived in Baysdale. Nan Hardwicke, who lived near Danby, would squat among the heather and the local lads would flush her out with hounds and chase her, but they never caught her; and there is an account of Nan visiting a relation in Farndale, twenty miles away: to cover the journey quickly, she changed into a hare. Nanny Pearson of Goathland was said to turn herself into a hare and one day was shot with silver by a man courting the squire's daughter. The hare was not killed, but next day Nanny was seen with corresponding injuries.

One form of advice was that if a witch-hare was caught, it should be shod, and the shoes would remain fixed to the hands of the witch when she resumed human form.

But there is one account in which a witch-hare outwitted her attacker. At Westerdale a witch-hare known in its human form as Awd Mally was supposedly stealing milk, so a farmer laid in wait with his gun. It was loaded with the necessary silver shot made from old buttons, for the farmer intended catching her in the act. But instead of stealing the milk, she attacked him! The account says, 'She cem at him wiv her een glooring and widening while they were as big as saucers.' Terrified, he threw his gun away and locked himself inside his house.

There is one story of a witch in Farndale turning herself into a black dog. A worried farmer noticed that whenever a certain black bitch was around his cowshed, one of his cows became ill and eventually died. After taking advice, he decided it was a witch using the form of a dog for her nefarious activities, so he loaded his gun with silver shot and waited. At night, the black dog arrived and attempted to gain entry to the calves' pen, but it failed. As it was leaving, he opened fire and scored a hit, whereupon the dog ran off injured. Next day, he called at the home of the local witch and found her ill in bed with severe gunshot wounds to her hind quarters.

There is little doubt that lonely old women, or those who were odd in any way, were cast as witches in the eyes of the superstitious moorfolk. It was comparatively simple to weave acceptable stories about them, stories which over the years have become more and more exaggerated. Some of those old ladies have been named, and their names survive to this day in local folklore and old accounts.

The named witches of the Moors include Awd Kathy o' Ruswarp, Nan Scaife o' Spaunton Moor, who used a magic cube, Awd Mother Migg o' Cropton, who used a crystal, Sally Craggs o' Allerston, who could change herself into a cat, Esther Mudd o' Rosedale, who used the evil eye, Nanny Pierson o' Goathland, who could turn herself into a hare, Emma Todd o' Ebberston, who was well off in matters of the black arts, Nancy Nairs o' Pickering, who used a crystal, Peggy Devell o' Hutton-le-Hole, who used a magic book, and Awd Jeannie o' Mulgrave, who terrified the local people with her spells and incantations.

In some accounts, Jeannie was a good fairy with a fearsome temper when upset. In either tale, she was so troublesome to the farmers that one of them decided to put an end to her. He rode to her home in Hob's Cave at Mulgrave, but as he approached, she darted furiously at him, and in spite of his brave promises he turned tail and fled. She gave chase with a wand; the faster he rode, the faster she flew behind, turning into a horrible, ugly creature who called out terrifying threats. She began to gain and had almost reached him when he leapt his horse over a stream. Fairies could not cross water, so she brought down her wand and cut his horse in two. But he just managed to reach the safety of the far side of the river.

One can imagine this tale being told and re-told on dark nights as the winds of winter howled around, with the combined imaginations of listeners and story-teller giving it a fearful reality.

The tales show how deeply the folks of the Moors believed in the evil of witches, especially as they affected their livestock and domestic lives. Many farms and cottages would be adorned with charms to ward off the witches, and these included horseshoes, crosses made of hazel wood, horsebrasses, stones with holes in them, corn dollies, witch bottles buried in the thresholds, and twigs of rowan or elderberry trees planted near the cattlesheds.

Among the devices used to ward off witches were witch-posts, and an example of these can be seen in the Ryedale Folk Museum at Hutton-le-Hole. A witch-post is an upright piece of timber, usually from the rowan tree, which forms part of the structure of the fireplace in primitive moorland homes. It often supported one end of the smoke-hood and was identified by the cross carved on its face close to the top. Some of the existing ones bear a simple X mark, while others have symbolic carvings around the X.

It is an odd fact that, with one exception, witch-posts are found only in a small area of the North York Moors. (The exception is one discovered at Rawtenstall, in Lancashire.) Those known to have existed (and which still exist) have been recorded at Danby, Glaisdale, Rosedale, Gillamoor, Farndale, Egton and Lealholm, with two near Scarborough. Several are now in museums, although some remain in position in old, but occupied moorland homes.

Their purpose has been disputed by some folklorists but the general belief is that they were installed to ward off the evil machinations of local witches, the cross upon them being the device employed. One theory is that a local priest, after 'laying the witch', actually carved the cross as proof that the household in question had been placed beyond the power of future witches. Indeed, these posts were once known as priests' posts, the X being the mark of a particular priest. As these have been found in such a localized area, generally very close to Eskdale, there is a theory that they are the work of one travelling priest, who may also have visited Lancashire.

Another weird charm associated with Eskdale is the infamous and ghastly Hand of Glory. This was used by superstitious criminals as late as 1831, and it was a real hand, taken from the corpse of a man hanged on the gibbet. Once severed, it was cured as one might cure a piece of ham. A candle of human fat, wax and Lapland sesame was placed between the fingers, the wick fashioned from human hair, also taken from a hanged man.

The Hand of Glory was now ready for use. When the candle was lit, it was believed the Hand had the ability to make sleeping persons remain asleep and waking persons remain awake – so that a thief could work without fear of disturbance. For the charm to be effective, however, a verbal ritual had to be undergone before the thief could search for the loot. Once he was inside the house or inn, he would light his candle and incant these lines:

Let those who rest more deeply sleep,
Let those awake their vigils keep,
Oh, Hand of Glory, shed thy light –
Direct us to our spoils tonight.

Then, as the weird light filled the room, other lines followed:

Flash out thy blaze, oh skeleton hand,
And guide the feet of our trusty band.
Let those who are awake remain awake,
And those who are asleep keep asleep.

Sight of the flame was said to paralyse anyone except the owners, and only when the flame was extinguished was the spell broken. And the flame could be extinguished by one of only two liquids, milk or blood.

For burglars and robbers of wayside inns, the Hand of Glory was therefore a marvellous and much-sought-after charm, as it would compel their victims to remain asleep as their property was ransacked. So gibbets were regularly raided by criminals who hunted the materials for these Hands.

There are stories of their use in the North Riding of Yorkshire, one of them dated the winter of 1790. One of these Hands, known as the Danby Hand of Glory is now in Pannett Museum at Whitby.

It follows that a rural area of this nature, with all its deep superstitions, is also replete with legends. These follow the general pattern of many others, for they comprise tales of lost or found wealth, or lost and found lovers, and fights with dragons, often with a moral message hidden within the tale.

Two of which deal with treasure are the tale of Awd Nan of Sexhow, and the Crock of Upsall Gold.

A farmer who lived at Sexhow near Stokesley was visited one night by the ghost of Awd Nan, a local woman. She said that an apple tree in his orchard grew above a chest of gold and silver and that she would reveal its hiding-place. There was a condition, however: he could keep all the silver, but the gold had to be handed over to her niece, who lived in poverty. The farmer agreed and the precise plan was revealed. When he dug deep, he found the chest and carried it indoors to find a wonderful treasure. But greed overcame him. He decided that, as it had been buried in his land and he had unearthed it, it all belonged to him. He would not give the gold to Awd Nan's niece. From that time, everything went wrong. His farm and his health failed, and he turned to drink. Then one night, as he rode home from the inn, the ghost of Awd Nan followed him and chased him. By now, he was shouting, 'I will, I will, I will,' but he tried to leap the gate into his farmyard. His horse fell, and he died from his injuries. One account says that the black form of the ghostly witch clung to the poor farmer's back as he rode to escape her!

The other story tells of a poor man who lived at Upsall, near Thirsk. He dreamt that if he stood on London Bridge, he would learn something to his advantage, and as the dream recurred on three successive nights, he decided to make the long trip from the Moors to London. He went all the way on foot, well over two hundred miles.

As he stood for hours on London Bridge without anyone speaking to him, he began to think he was an utter fool. But then a stranger bade him good-day, and they fell into conversation. He began to tell the stranger of his peculiar dream, whereupon the man interrupted him before the whole story emerged and said, 'Now that's odd. I had a dream too. Last night, I dreamt I had found a crock of gold under an elderberry bush in the grounds of Upsall Castle. And I've never heard of the place!'

The canny Yorkshireman did not reveal that he knew Upsall, but returned and began to dig. Sure enough, he found a crock of gold, but the lid bore a curious inscription that he could not understand. No one else in Upsall could translate it, and so it was kept in the local inn as a curio. Then a Jew chanced to stay there one night, noticed the lid and immediately understood it. It said, 'Look lower; where this stood is another twice as good.' Our hero went back, dug again and found another crock with the same inscription, and a third session of digging produced a third crock of gold. Now he had enough to last him the rest of his life.

There are three 'George and Dragon' type stories associated with the Moors, and each follows the traditional pattern of knight versus dragon, or perhaps good versus evil.

One is based upon Handale, a location on the northern boundary of the National Park, near Loftus. This well-wooded district boasted a Benedictine nunnery in 1133, but the legend says a dragon lived in the woods. Like most of these creatures, this one kidnapped young girls for its meals. It attracted them by its eyes; when it gazed into a girl's eyes, she was compelled to follow, and no one dared approach its lair in an attempt to rescue her or kill the beast, which became known as the Serpent of Handale.

And then, as in all good stories, a brave youth came to Handale determined to put a stop to the Serpent's evil ways. His name was Scaw, and he obtained a suit of armour and a sword before setting out to locate the Serpent's lair. It was inside, hissing horribly, and as Scaw approached, it leapt out. With a terrible roar, it attacked him, its huge tail demolishing trees, and its fiery breath scorching his armour. But the brave youth went closer, sword at the ready, and, as in all good yarns, he 'smote' it. He smote it time and time again, his armour growing so hot that he almost collapsed, but finally it plunged its fiery head towards him and he managed to thrust his blade down its throat. Thus he killed the Serpent of Handale.

He cut off the head, just to be sure, and then entered the cave. Inside was a beautiful and terrified maiden with whom he fell hopelessly in love. She happened to be the daughter of a wealthy lord, and so the brave Scaw married her and lived happily ever after. In Handale Priory long ago, there was a stone coffin said to contain the body of the mighty Scaw, while a nearby copse was called Scaw Wood in his honour.

The second story involves Sexhow, already mentioned in the Awd Nan tale. About a mile outside the National Park boundary, Sexhow had a small, round hill where a dragon came to live. It fed exclusively on milk, requiring nine cows every day to keep it supplied, and when the supply failed, the dragon breathed poisonous fumes across the countryside. This caused crops to fail and livestock to die, and the angry dragon was depopulating the area. Along came an unknown knight, who, in passing through Sexhow, slew the dragon and passed on. No one knows who he was, but the skin of the slain dragon was hung inside the church to remind the villagers of their deliverance.

The third story tells how Sir Peter Loschy of Nunnington fought the feared Nunnington Worm, which breathed fire and smoke. It also had a poisoned tongue and teeth as big as the prongs of a pitchfork. It had killed many local damsels and brave knights, but Sir Peter thought he had the answer to the problem. He made a suit of armour covered in razor blades and set off in pursuit of the Worm. It wrapped itself around him and cut itself into hundreds of small pieces, but as each fell to the ground, it magically restored itself. He fought it for more than two hours, using his sword to chop it into smaller pieces, but as soon as Sir Peter severed a piece, it joined itself together again. And like a good knight, he smote it repeatedly.

But Sir Peter had a wonderful little dog, and as he tired from his weary fight, he whistled for it and the dog dashed into the fray. As Sir Peter chopped off a piece of the giant Worm, the dog seized it and galloped off. It dumped the piece far away. It returned for more, and Sir Peter obliged until there was only the Worm's head left. By now, it was dead, and the gallant little dog carried the head to a hill near Nunnington Church. The awful battle was over, and the people of Nunnington were rid of the horror which had threatened them for so long.

Sir Peter bent down to pat his little dog, and it jumped up and licked his face, but on its tongue was some of the poison from the Worm, and Sir Peter fell dead at that instant. It is said that his dog died shortly afterwards from sorrow. If you enter

Nunnington's lovely old church, you will see an ancient tomb with a stone figure of a knight in armour upon it. And at the feet of this figure is a small dog.

One of the most poignant love stories from the Moors is told in the legend of Sarkless Kitty. Kitty was a pretty girl from Farndale who fell in love with a rich farmer's son. Everyone hoped they would marry, but unfortunately, before the wedding, Kitty found she was pregnant. When her lover found out, he discarded her and would not even speak to her. Sad and disillusioned, Kitty pleaded with him, and at last he consented to meet her for one last time. This made Kitty full of hope. She felt that their love would be re-kindled if only they could talk privately, and so she waited that evening at the appointed place and time.

But poor Kitty waited and waited. There was no sign of her lover. And then she learned that the River Dove was in flood. Perhaps he could not cross the raging river? She went towards the ford, but on the way she met a horseman who said he had earlier seen a rider, believed to be Kitty's lover, riding in the opposite direction, into Kirkbymoorside. This was the last straw. Now totally disillusioned and believing she had been cruelly betrayed, Kitty stood by the side of the raging torrent, removed all her clothes ('sark an' all' as the story says) and leapt into the flood waters.

Her sad drowned body was found later near the old ford at the foot of Farndale, and it lay beside that of her lover, who had perished in the same flood. Tragically, he had ridden into Kirkbymoorside to buy a ring and had drowned on the way back to greet her with his undying love. As was the custom, they were buried at the roadside because it was thought they had committed suicide. From that time, the ghost of Sarkless Kitty haunted that locality every year on the anniversary of her death.

When the river claimed another victim, this caused terrible worries among the local people, and they began to wonder how they could halt this annual toll of death. Living nearby was a Quaker couple, also worried about this awful sequence of events, and after a vivid dream the Quaker gentleman and his wife went secretly to the riverside and exhumed the bodies of Kitty and her lover. Their remains were decently buried in a nearby Quaker burial ground, and from that time the hauntings and deaths ceased. Kitty and her lover were finally at peace.

Stories and superstitious beliefs of this kind have been part of the life of the Moors for generations, and even today remnants of this dark, superstitious past remain.

On New Year's Day, the tradition of First Footing is carried out in many homes, its purpose being to bring good fortune. A tall, dark man must be first into one's home in the New Year, arriving as soon after midnight as possible, and he must carry a piece of bread or coal and some salt or money, which symbolize the necessities of life, and sometimes an evergreen like holly is included, a symbol of everlasting life. The First Footer must always be male, never flat-footed or cross-eyed, and his eyebrows must not meet. If he is a total stranger who meets these requirements and enters one's home, then one's luck is immensely enhanced.

In some houses, the fire is never let out over New Year's Eve and into New Year's Day, and even the ashes are not removed on New Year's Day, a relic of the times when fire was a precious commodity. It was thought that if the fire burned as New Year arrived, fire would be plentiful over the coming twelve months. To extinguish a fire or remove it was tantamount to cutting off one's lifeline.

The custom of April Fool's Day continues, with youngsters endeavouring to make gentle fools of their friends or parents until noon, and on 1 May a similar prank known as May Gosling is perpetrated.

The birth of a baby continues to evoke memories of the Dark Ages, for it is customary to give a newborn child a silver coin upon first seeing it to ensure luck during its life. Another fading custom followed a christening: the first person seen after the ceremony had to be given a piece of bread and cheese by the baby's family, to ensure luck.

Weddings bring out their traditions too, such as when coins are thrown to the bystanders, and the bride fearing to wear anything green.

Snowdrops are never allowed in some homes because they bring death; a robin, even a seasonal picture of one on a Christmas card, is unwelcome indoors for the same reason. Trees like the elderberry and mountain ash or rowan were encouraged near the house to ward off witches, and Hallowe'en is still a time for witches to be abroad in the form of children wearing masks and carrying turnip lanterns.

The superstition attached to the sight of magpies is very much alive, with the old verse still being quoted,

One for sorrow, two for joy,
Three for a girl and four for a boy,
Five is for silver, six is for gold,
Seven's a secret never to be told.
Eight is for a wish and nine for a kiss,
With ten for a marriage never to be old.

On 4 November, Mischief Night is still practised, when the idea is to play harmless pranks upon friends and neighbours, but sadly this has degenerated lately into an excuse for committing vandalism and damage. Bonfire Night, now known as Guy Fawkes' Night, is another relic of time long past when fires were lit in the late autumn to compensate for the loss of the life-giving sun during the long winter.

There are many other customs, far too many to chronicle here, but old men still turn over the money in their pockets at the sound of the first cuckoo, and some mothers refuse to cut the nails of new-born babies – they bite them off instead. Knives are never given as presents, and the new moon is not looked at through glass. Luck money is still handed over during sales at cattle markets, potatoes are planted on Good Friday, and new brides are carried over the threshold of their new homes.

Another survival within the Moors is the distinctive dialect of the region. It was Robert Southey in *The Doctor* who wrote that, 'He spoke the King's English in one circle and the King's Yorkshire in another.' And so it is with many moorland folk. Many of them are bilingual, speaking English with a North York Moors accent when the occasion demands, but turning to their dialect when among family, friends and colleagues.

Accent and dialect are very different indeed. Most of the inhabitants of this island speak English with an accent of some kind, but few speak in a true dialect whose origins go back to the Vikings or even beyond. There are many glossaries of the North Riding dialect, and indeed glossaries of those from small areas, for even within the Moors there are many differing dialects. Staithes, on the coast, for example, has its own, while each of the dales differs in some way from its neighbours. It requires a sharp ear to determine those differences, but they do exist.

The people of the Moors take a tremendous pride in their native tongue, with all its local variations. It is a distinctive language in its own right, with its own vocabulary, while the conjugation of its verbs and its composite usage follow the grammatical patterns of most European tongues.

The first real study of the dialect was undertaken by William Marshall of Pickering, the noted agriculturist. (He originated the idea of the National Board of Agriculture which was put into effect by Parliament in 1793. This was later to become the Ministry of Agriculture, Fisheries and Food.) In 1788 Marshall published a glossary of the North Riding dialect comprising a thousand words or so, and this earned him praise as 'The Father of All the Glossaries of the North Riding Dialect'. Marshall, a widely travelled and brilliant man, died in 1818 and is buried at Pickering.

John Castillo was another dialect writer who is buried at Pickering, and he was working around the same time as Marshall. A stonemason by trade, he lived in Eskdale and wrote poetry in dialect, often recording his travels across the Moors as he preached his fiery brand of Methodism. He died in 1845. His book of poems survives in many moorland homes, including my own. It is called *Bard of the Dales*.

Many other dialect writers followed, some compiling learned glossaries, others preferring humour, plays or poetry, but all using the ancient tongue of the Moors. Over the years, many of its words have disappeared but because dialect is a living language, new words arrive and so the speech survives.

None the less, it is struggling for survival, because modern youngsters travel widely, they talk with others who do not use the dialect, they watch TV and listen to the radio, all of which make difficulties in the use of dialect. Standard English must be used to make oneself understood, even if it is spoken with a North Yorkshire accent.

But in the deep dales and moors, the older folk continue with their delightful tongue, and take pleasure in baffling visitors and tourists with the use of curious words and phrases. In the local inns, they will deliberately make use of the more unusual aspects of their dialect, bringing out words like yottening, prink, mistetch, glishy, keslip, gomerill, fegs, brussen, kist, routering-time and so on. They'll call a garden fork a gripe, and use 'graithing' to refer to the repair of a plough, while someone who has over-eaten is 'kedged'.

In some areas, sheep were counted with an almost musical lilt in the words, 'Yan, tan, tethera, pethera, pimp, saffra, laffra, ofra, doffra, dix. Ena dix, tena dix, tethera dix, pethera dix, bumpit, ena bumpit, tena bumpit, tethera bumpit, pethera bumpit, siggit.' That is the sequence from one to twenty, but these words do vary across the moors, and are no longer in common use.

It is impossible to convey the true sound of dialect in the written form, because many of its words are phonetic, and it needs a true dialect-speaker to pronounce them correctly and to understand the inflections.

There is a lovely tale of a farmer explaining to a doctor how he'd hurt his back as he carted 't'laud o' manner' from his farmyard. The doctor thought he was referring to the Lord of the Manor, and this puzzled him immensely, but in fact the farmer was talking about a load of manure.

For those who might wish to understand the story of the hob on page 169 or the witch-hare on page 174, here is a glossary of some words from those stories.

Swipple – the swinging or striking part of a flail; yah or yan – one; gannan – going; bat – stroke; lathe – barn; fleear – floor; ken – know; wad – would; deea – do or sometimes day; mair – more; gat – got; hissel – himself; croppen – crept; anenst – close to, nearby; deear – door; leeaked – looked; thruff – through; lahtle – little or small; spangin' – striking around, lashing out; fleeal – flail; lahk – like; haill – whole, entire; dess – layer, heap; shaffs – sheaves; tonned oot – turned out; strae – straw; sided away – cleared up; rife – ready; neea – no; mak or mander o' duds – style or fashion of clothes; aud or awd – old; sark – rough working shirt; hap – to enclose, wrap; hamp – a loose working cover or shirt; berry – thresh; stamp – knocking off the beards of barley prior to threshing it; heear – hare; knepping – nipping off in small quantities, nibbling; maist – most; tahm – time; sae – so; lat – let; dhrive – drive; flaysome – frightful; skrike – scream, shriek; sair hot – badly hurt; nossery – nursery; heeam – home; scroggs – stunted brushwood.

10

Posctscript

Since 'tis nature's law to change,
Constancy alone is strange.
John Wilmot, Earl of Rochester (1647–80)

From their quiet corner in the north-east of Yorkshire, the North York Moors have enjoyed a long and honourable history. With traditional rural modesty, they have played a significant role in our nation's development, their achievements ranging from man's first flight to the creation of English poetry, by way of calculating the date of Easter in addition to other contributions to our religious and cultural heritage.

The natural reticence of the people who live and work there has kept to a minimum any unseemly boasting of these accomplishments: therefore it falls to historians and to the future to assess their impact and value. Meanwhile, the people of the Moors continue to live and work in their spectacular surroundings, at times resisting progress and change, and believing, I am sure, that neither progress nor change necessarily produces improvement.

But progress and change cannot be halted, while improvement can result only from a concerted and studied effort by many people and organizations. But what is thought to be an improvement in one person's mind is not necessarily an improvement in the mind of others. Examples of this can be seen in the sculpture on East Moors above Helmsley, the towering globes of Fylingdales Ballistic Missile Early Warning Station and some formally approved buildings which have appeared in moorland villages.

Time cannot stand still. The Moors, like any other area of Great Britain, must adjust to changing attitudes and practices, and in some ways this has been thrust upon them due to their own distinctive charm and beauty. Understandably, people from afar and people from cities and large conurbations wish to experience the joys of this rural haven, if only for a short time. Furthermore, they are prepared to travel many miles and to spend large sums of money in order to do so and to partake of a way of life the moorland folk have for generations taken for granted.

This influx of visitors has been gradual. It began long ago in the coastal resorts of Scarborough and Whitby: then, due largely to the motor car, it spread into the dales and villages, then onto the moors. Villages which seldom saw an outsider began to witness carloads and coachloads of them, and as those visitors broadcast their impressions, more of them came to savour these delights.

Within the last twenty years or even less, I have seen the impact of the visitor upon many small moorland communities. It is difficult to determine the precise moment that mass tourism came to the moorlands, but its effect has been manifold. This is not to say that tourism is a bad thing – it is not, for it has resulted in fresh enterprise and the creation of many new businesses in areas which might otherwise have become derelict and devoid of a population.

Among the more common, visible effects are the widening of our roads, the appearance of yellow 'No Parking' lines in some villages, the proliferation of signs and notices, the construction of car-parks and toilet blocks, the menace of litter, the arrival of small shops and restaurants and the increase of seldom-used holiday cottages.

While agriculture has always been the main source of occupation for the moorland people, it remains so, but today it is combined with tourism. Caravan and camping sites are appearing on land which hitherto had been valueless: bed-and-breakfast facilities are available in many farmhouses and cottages: and those people engaged in agriculture are now able to expand their enterprises by serving the tourists with their home-grown produce.

This, therefore, is the new Klondike of the Moors. Other Klondikes have come and gone: we've had the whaling of Whitby, the ironstone boom of the dales, the jet industry, the mining of alum and the building of railways. All have left their mark, and in their times all produced work, jobs and money for the moorland people.

Tourism is now fulfilling that role but it is not for me to anticipate whether this Klondike will ever end. It is sufficient to say that it has arrived and that the moorfolk, as well as their colleagues along the coastline, are taking full advantage of it. Some are leaving their traditional work to cater full-time for the tourists, and others, like the farmers and fishermen, are using the influx of visitors as a means of expanding their existing enterprises.

But not all those who are taking advantage of the opportunities are resident moorfolk. Enterprising outsiders are moving in; they are buying cottages, opening shops, boutiques, restaurants and other tourist-related businesses. But it cannot and must not be said that such incomers are taking business away from the local people. Indeed, it is distinctly possible they are drawing in revenue which filters back to the local people in direct or indirect ways, and there is no doubt that many enthusiastic operators are now providing employment for young people who would otherwise move from the area.

But the point is that moors people, young and old, are having to turn away from their traditional rural or agricultural outlook. They need to seek employment either away from the Moors or in work which has resulted from the changes forced upon them by their very surroundings.

None the less, many older occupations remain – there will always be the village shopkeeper, tradesmen of all kinds, innkeepers and small business people. They remain to fulfil the village function that has always been their responsibility.

It must not be thought, either, that tourism is the sole source of finance or occupation in and around the Moors. Some of our local craftsmen and business people are known locally, nationally and even internationally and cater for a clientele far removed from occasional visitors. Salesmen live and work in the Moors, and there are numerous governmental and local authority workers, with all the attendant service industries. The Moors and the people could exist without tourism, but tourism does provide very welcome benefits.

But while tourism has wrought these changes and made such an impact upon the villages and dales, the Moors themselves are undergoing a change – a change which puts them at grave risk of disappearing in their present form. It is very gradual and barely evident to the casual eye, but just as the majesty of nature has produced such a beautiful area, that same power is threatening the very moors which dominate this district.

It has already been said in these pages that the Moors are under constant risk of destruction by fire and that the regular pounding of hikers' boots is causing concern. But there is further anxiety because the heather itself is in jeopardy. Currently the North York Moors form England's largest area of open heather-covered moorland, and this is maintained by a delicate balance of nature. That balance is vital – if it was upset, the heather could disappear and bracken replace it – and bracken is almost impervious to attempts to remove it. This means that, if we wish to maintain this unique heather-covered area of upland, we must ensure that all the required stimuli remain.

One of those comes in the shape of moorland sheep, and another is the indigenous grouse. Landowners are finding that the maintenance of their grouse moors is becoming increasingly expensive, and the anti-shooting militants are not helping by making grouse-shooting more difficult and more expensive. If the grouse disappears, the heather will suffer. Similarly, the absence of grazing moorland sheep will mean that the heather gives way to the ever-encroaching bracken.

As things are, sheep farmers and grouse moor owners regularly encourage strong, new heather by controlled burning, and they do this so that the grouse and the sheep will flourish. With no sheep or grouse to nurture, the heather will be left to its own devices, which means the bracken will triumph. Even now, it is triumphing to the extent of covering thousands of new acres per year.

But why should there be concern about the disappearance of the sheep? To take one area in isolation, in 1959 the number of sheep grazing on open moorland along the Whitby to Pickering road numbered about four thousand. Today it is about two thousand, and of those fifteen per cent (around three hundred) are killed annually by motor vehicles. There is a stage at which the rearing of moorland sheep becomes uneconomic, and with such a dreadful toll at the wheels of motorists, the sheep farmer is beginning to wonder whether his efforts are worthwhile.

Fencing in the moors has preserved the lives of many animals, but this causes protests from visitors who feel that the Moors belong to Everyman. They don't, of course; they are largely privately owned, but landowners have, over the years, allowed almost unrestricted access. But if Everyman drove his car with a little more care, it would be unnecessary to fence in the sheep, and Everyman could continue to feel the spring of the heather beneath his city boots.

So, if the farmers abandon their moorland sheep-rearing operations, and if grouse-shooting disappears from these heights, the heather will surely vanish beneath a sea of indestructible bracken. Happily, as reported in these pages, work is being undertaken to find a way of controlling bracken, and the Moors are one of the test areas.

But it is not just the bracken which threatens it. Over the last twenty-five years, one quarter of the moorland area has been reclaimed for agricultural purposes. This land is now fenced off and no longer qualifies as 'moorland'.

There is acid rain too. A survey published in September 1984 showed that it is sufficiently strong in the North York Moors to cause irritation to the skin of human beings.

It is no consolation to remind ourselves that within the span of mankind there was no heather on these moors. They were covered with deciduous forests, and it was the untrained husbandry of early man which removed the woodland and made room for the heather. It would be strange if man's neglect of those same moors obliterated that heather and obliterated the characteristics we love so much.

But such is the onward march of progress; changes are inevitable, and nature is the initiator of many. It is hoped that the people of the Moors can cope with the changes that are now occurring in addition to those which will inevitably occur in the future.

It is my own earnest desire that the North York Moors, with their magnificent covering of purple heather, their outstanding views, their beautiful dales and surviving way of life, will remain for ever, and that the people who live and work among them will strive towards that end.

Let us all hope that the words of St Augustine do not ring true, for he said, 'Too late came I to love thee, O thou beauty both so ancient and so fresh. Yea, too late came I to love thee.'

Bibliography

The following publications have been invaluable during my research for this book:

On the North York Moors

The North York Moors, Stanhope White (Dalesman Publications, 1979)

Inside the North York Moors, Harry Mead (David & Charles, 1978)

Life in the Moorlands of North-East Yorkshire, Marie Hartley and Joan Ingilby (J.M.Dent & Sons, 1972)

North York Moors – A Dalesman Guide (Dalesman Publications, 1982)

The North York Moors National Park, Dr A. Raistrick (Ed.) (HMSO, 1966)

The North York Moors (North York Moors National Park Committee, 1981)

North Yorkshire Forests, H.L.Edlin (Ed.) (HMSO, 1963)

Dalesman Guide to the North York Moors (Dalesman Publishing Company, 1982)

Legends of the North York Moors, Marion Atkinson (Dalesman Books, 1981)

Wild Life of the North York Moors, Ian Carstairs (Studio Print, Great Ayton, 1983)

On the North Riding

The Early History of the North Riding, William Edwards (A.Brown & Sons Ltd, 1924)

Yorkshire, North Riding, Arthur Mee (Hodder & Stoughton, revised edition 1970)

The Placenames of the North Riding of Yorkshire, A.H.Smith (Cambridge University Press, 1928)

Fair North Riding, Alfred J. Brown (Country Life Ltd, 1952)
Companion into the North Riding, J.H.Ingram (Methuen & Co Ltd, 1952)
The North Riding of Yorkshire, Joseph E.Morris (Methuen & Co Ltd, 1920)
Yorkshire, North Riding, Oswald Harland (Robert Hale Ltd, 1951)
A Dictionary of North Riding Dialect, Sir Alfred Pease (Horne & Son Ltd, 1928)

On Local History
A History of Helmsley, Rievaulx and District, J.McDonnell (Ed.) (Stonegate Press, York, 1963)
Whitby Lore and Legend, Percy Shaw Jeffrey (Horne & Son, 1952)
Romantic Ryedale, Bill and Joan Spence (Ryedale Printers, 1977)
Forty Years on a Moorland Parish, J.C.Atkinson (MacMillan & Co Ltd, 1908)
Wade's Causeway, R.H.Hayes and J.G.Rutter (Scarborough Archaeological & Historical Society, 1964)
A History of Rosedale, R.H.Hayes (Ryedale Printing Works, 1973)
Some Reminiscences and Folklore of Danby Parish and District, Joseph Ford (Horne & Son Ltd, 1953)
Ampleforth Country, Students of Ampleforth College (Herald Printers, York, 1966)
Queen of the Dales, George Harland (Horne & Son, 1970)
The Whitby and Pickering Railway, David Joy (Dalesman Publications, 1969)
Bits of West Cleveland, J.Fairfax-Blakeborough (T.Woolston, 1901)

On Yorkshire as a Whole
Handbook for Travellers in Yorkshire, John Murray (Murray, London, 1874)
A Picturesque History of Yorkshire J.S.Fletcher, three volumes (J.M.Dent & Sons, 1901)
Striding through Yorkshire, Alfred J.Brown (Country Life Ltd, 1945)

General Reading

Roman Britain, Keith Branigan (Readers' Digest Association Ltd, 1980)

The Romans in Yorkshire, Dr A. Raistrick (Dalesman Publications, 1965)

Castles and Abbeys of Yorkshire, William Grainge (Whittaker & Co, 1855)

Bygone Yorkshire, William Andrews (A.Brown & Sons 1892)

Secret Rooms of Yorkshire, Winifred Haward (Dalesman Publications, 1956)

The Yorkshire Coast, John Leyland (Seeley & Co, 1892)

The Yorkshire Coast (Ward Lock Red Guides, Ward Lock & Co Ltd)

Rambles by Yorkshire Rivers, George Radford (R.Jackson, Leeds)

The Lyke Wake Walk, Bill Cowley (Dalesman Books, 1962)

The Cleveland Way, Alan Falconer (HMSO, 1972)

Domestic Folklore, Rev.T.F.Thistleton Dyer (Cassell, Petter, Galpin & Co, 1881)

Folklore of the Northern Counties, William Henderson (Longman, Green & Co, 1866)

Yorkshire Legends and Traditions, Thomas Parkinson (Elliot Stock, 1888)

Yorkshire Legend and Folklore, John R.Crossland (Collins, 1931)

Legendary Yorkshire, Frederick Ross (William Andrews & Co, 1892)

Yorkshire Wit, Character, Folklore and Custom, Richard Blakeborough (W.Rapp & Sons, 1898)

With Dickens in Yorkshire, T.P.Cooper (Ben Johnson Ltd, 1923)

Bard of the Dales, John Castillo (W.F.Pratt, Stokesley, 1858)

The Life of Laurence Sterne, Percy FitzGerald (Chatto & Windus, 1905)

Canon J.L.Kyle, MA, Vicar of Carlton-in-Cleveland, J.Fairfax-Blakeborough (Published by the author, 1968)

The Courts of Law, Peter N.Walker (David & Charles, 1970)

Index

Index